W9-DIH-592

Workplace Education
for
Low-Wage Workers

Workplace Education
for
Low-Wage Workers

Amanda L. Ahlstrand
Laurie J. Bassi
and
Daniel P. McMurrer

2003

W.E. Upjohn Institute for Employment Research
Kalamazoo, Michigan

Library of Congress Cataloging-in-Publication Data

Ahlstrand, Amanda L.
  Workplace education for low-wage workers / Amanda L. Ahlstrand, Laurie
J. Bassi, Daniel P. McMurrer.
    p. cm.
  Includes bibliographical references and index.
  ISBN 0-88099-265-4 (pbk. : alk. paper) — ISBN 0-88099-266-2 (cloth :
alk. paper)
  1. Employer-supported education—United States. 2.
Employees—Education–United States—Case studies. 3. Employee
assistance programs—United States—Case studies. 4. Working
class—Education—United States. I. Bassi, Laurie J. (Laurie Jo), 1954-
II. McMurrer, Daniel P. III. Title
  HF5549.5.T7A36 2003
  331.25'92'0973—dc21

                                    2003010838

W.E. Upjohn Institute for Employment Research
300 S. Westnedge Avenue
Kalamazoo, Michigan 49007–4686

The facts presented in this study and the observations and viewpoints expressed are
the sole responsibility of the authors. They do not necessarily represent positions of
the W.E. Upjohn Institute for Employment Research.

Cover design by J.R. Underhill
Index prepared by Diane Worden.
Printed in the United States of America.
Printed on recycled paper.

Contents

Tables

Acknowledgments

The authors gratefully acknowledge the support of grants to the American Society for Training and Development (ASTD) from the Ford Foundation and the W.E. Upjohn Institute for Employment Research, which jointly made this research project possible. John Colborn at the Ford Foundation and Kevin Hollenbeck at the Upjohn Institute provided invaluable guidance and suggestions, shaping the focus of our research. Kevin also played an integral and supportive role in preparing the manuscript for publication.

The members of our advisory board—James DeVito, David Ellwood, Robert Lerman, Beth Shulman, and James Van Erden—generously shared their valuable time and insights, helping to steer and focus the project during its development, and remaining available to advise us throughout the effort.

Others at ASTD and elsewhere played various important roles in the research. We especially wish to thank Max Armbruster for his contribution to Chapter 4, Bill Woodwell for his writing assistance on Chapter 11, and Katherine Dols for editing an early version of the work. The interviews that Julie Ruggles did as part of our research for the Ford Foundation were particularly influential in helping us to understand the policy implications of our findings. Throughout the project, Mark Van Buren, ASTD's director of research, provided priceless support, suggestions, and encouragement. We also thank three anonymous reviewers for their helpful insights, and Frances Emery for her superb job editing the final manuscript.

The project included eight case-study site visits, seven of which are reported in this book. These would not have been possible without the cooperation and hospitality of our main contacts at the organizations we visited— Cynthia Farrell, Susan Gregory, Jill Larkin, Tracy Laurie, Val Rodekhar, Kari Rosentrater, Joe Singer, and Jerry Spruiel. With the help of many of their colleagues, these eight individuals worked hard to ensure that we would have the information and access necessary to develop a true understanding of their organizations and their training strategies and philosophies. They spent hours speaking with us, and also provided extensive opportunities to conduct private interviews with lower-wage workers, executives, and managers throughout their organizations.

Finally, we thank the many organizations that shared their time and experiences with us through their participation in the telephone surveys conducted in the course of this research. Many of these organizations agreed to allow us to acknowledge their participation publicly; others preferred to remain anonymous. We list the publicly identified participating organizations in the discussion on telephone surveys in Chapter 2.

1
Introduction and Previous Research

The world economy is in the midst of a titanic shift. In comparison with their evolution from an agrarian to an industrial base, the world's now-developed economies have shifted from an industrial to a knowledge base with unprecedented speed. Nowhere is this more evident than in the United States. The remarkable flexibility exhibited by the U.S. economy has fueled its domination of the technology revolution, and has enabled that revolution to occur without catastrophic economic disruption. However, change of such magnitude and speed as the U.S. economy has recently undergone always produces some disruption.

Frequently, economic disruption takes the form of high unemployment. The U.S. economy, however, has experienced just the opposite. Although the United States is in the midst of a slowdown as this book goes to press, nonetheless its unemployment rates in recent years have been low by the standards of the past few decades.

This time, the expected disruption has come, instead, in the form of a slow but fairly steady decline in the inflation-adjusted wages of much of the workforce. Because of the extraordinary flexibility of the U.S. economy, these wage reductions have not reduced the standard of living for most households; families have supplemented falling wages by working longer hours and, in many cases, by adding a second wage earner.

Nevertheless, the decline in wages—particularly stark for those workers with the least formal education—is worrisome. The resultant increase in income inequality is the subject of inquiry and concern by both scholars and politicians. Increasingly, education is viewed as both the problem and the solution.

This study touches on these broader issues by examining a category of education and training that is not frequently put under the magnifying glass: employers' practices and decision-making processes with regard to workplace education and training for lower-wage workers. It is our hope that the results of the study will both inform public

1

policy and be of use to employers interested in enhancing the education and training that they provide to lower-wage workers.

THE NEED FOR WORKPLACE EDUCATION

Once people leave the education system, most—perhaps all—of their continuing education and training opportunities are provided through the workplace. Consequently, workplace education is critical if workers are to prosper in a rapidly changing economy. There are two sides to this equation. First, workplace education must be available. That is, there must be an adequate supply. Second, workers must see that it is in their interest to avail themselves of workplace education— that is, there must be demand. Although this is true for all workers, the availability of training opportunities, in the workplace and elsewhere, is particularly important for those workers near the bottom of the income distribution, especially those with low skill levels. These are the workers most likely to be "at risk" in the labor market, many of whom might benefit from significant workplace training opportunities.

For many such workers, however, useful workplace learning opportunities are not available. It is now a well-established research finding that the probability that workers will receive workplace education is directly proportional to their wage and education levels (see, for example, Frazis et al. 1998). Workers with the highest wages and the most formal education receive the most workplace education, while lower-wage workers and those with the lowest levels of education receive the least. This finding is problematic from a public policy perspective, since, as we discuss below, there is reason to believe that workplace education programs (which tend to be tied more closely to actual job requirements) may be more successful in raising earnings among lower-wage workers than are government-provided training programs.

It is clear that those workers who could benefit the most from workplace education are the least likely to get it. It is less clearly understood why lower-wage workers receive less workplace education. The supply side of the equation might be the cause: employers may not perceive it as being in their interest to provide opportunities for ongoing education for workers with fewer skills; they may perceive the benefits of training lower-wage workers to be low (perhaps because of higher turnover rate or lower average cognitive capability) or the costs high. Alternatively, the cause might be a dearth of demand: some (or many) lower-wage or lower-skill workers may not see it as in their interest to pursue such opportunities. The lack of demand may be a more significant obstacle among lower-wage workers than among the population as a whole, because many such workers already choose to curtail their participation in the formal education system at an earlier stage than the average worker. Perhaps the lack of both supply and demand for workplace education among lower-wage workers combine to bring about today's uneven distribution of workplace training.

LOWER-WAGE WORKERS

Lower-wage workers in the United States by no means form a homogenous group. They range from upwardly mobile college students working part-time to former welfare recipients entering the workforce for the first time. The lower-wage status of the former group is likely to be temporary and will be remedied naturally (as they mature, gain experience and additional education, and move from part-time, temporary work to full-time, permanent jobs). For them, a lack of workplace education opportunities may not represent a significant problem.

The same is not true, however, for other lower-wage workers—those whose lower-wage status is unlikely to be ameliorated simply by the passage of time. This group consists disproportionately of women, immigrants, and those with little formal education. For this latter group, a lack of opportunity or incentive to learn new skills at work does represent a significant problem.

Workers at the bottom of the earnings distribution are much less likely to receive education at work than are those with higher earnings. Data from the National Household Education Survey reveal, for example, that in 1995 only 22 percent of workers in the bottom quintile of the earnings distribution reported receiving employer-supported education during the previous year, whereas 40 percent of those in the top quintile reported receiving such training. Similar findings emerge when the data are tabulated by education level. Moreover, opportunities for informal training (as opposed to formal education and training, which are planned in advance with a specified curriculum) are also unequally available for workers with the least amount of formal education (Bassi 2000).

The best evidence on the impact of workplace education and training indicates that those workers who receive it earn significantly higher wages than comparable workers who do not receive education at work. For example, the wage rate benefit of 40 hours of workplace education is estimated to be 8 percent, which is as large as the return from an entire year of schooling (Frazis and Loewenstein 1999).

Among the needed educational interventions for those workers who are consistently at the bottom of the wage distribution, the most important seem to be courses in the following:

- basic skills, which are often necessary prerequisites for more advanced, job-specific training;
- English as a second language, for those who are not native English speakers;
- computer skills, since computer use is becoming an increasingly important predictor of wage levels; and
- problem-solving and interpersonal skills.

These findings suggest that the distribution of workplace education is a part of the problem. Although workplace education is a potential tool for helping to narrow the gap between those at the top and those at the bottom of the earnings distribution, it is, in fact, not serving that purpose. We might even conjecture that, rather than narrowing the wage gap, workplace education may well be a factor contributing to its growth.

EMPLOYERS OF LOWER-WAGE WORKERS

Given that employer-provided training is important in determining the earnings potential of employees, what factors determine whether employers choose to provide education and training to their employees? Economic theory predicts that, in fact, employers typically do not find it in their interest, in the absence of external incentives, to provide education and training for "general" skills that have broad applicability (Becker 1962). Yet the skills that are most likely to be needed by lower-wage workers fall into the general skills category.

Although there is substantial evidence (see below) that some employers do indeed provide and finance general training for their employees, Becker's theory serves to identify factors and disincentives that cause employers to provide less general education and training than they otherwise would. In particular, if an employer pays for education and training that raise an employee's productivity, then another employer, who did not have to pay for the training, will be able to offer the trained employee a higher wage. That is to say, economic theory predicts that employers who do provide generalized education and training will experience higher turnover as a result, and will be less profitable than employers who don't provide it. This prediction pertains to all types of workers, at both high and low wage levels.

Several strong assumptions serve as the foundation for this prediction: that labor markets are perfectly competitive; that the wage level is the only factor that determines employees' choice of an employer; and that employers can, in fact, "buy" the skills that they need by hiring workers with those skills. When the price of buying skills increases (either as a result of growing wage inequality or tight labor markets), there are more economic incentives for employers to choose instead to "make" skills, by providing more and better training to lower-wage workers. But the benefits to employers of doing so must exceed the costs. And as the theory outlined above suggests, underlying forces can make it difficult for employers to recover the investment that they make in general skills training, particularly if their workforce is subject to high turnover rates (as is often the case with lower-wage workers).

PREVIOUS RESEARCH

Gary Becker's seminal article on investment in human capital laid the foundation for the past four decades of economists' research on employer-provided education and training (Becker 1962). As noted above, an important insight that emerges from Becker's work is that in a highly competitive marketplace, employers will not find it in their interest to provide or finance general education and training (if we define "general education and training" as that which raises a worker's productivity for other employers to the same degree that it does for the employer who provided the training).

One obstacle that researchers have faced in exploring the hypotheses coming from Becker's worldview is the paucity of data that are well suited for testing the theory. In recent years, however, the quality of the data has improved. In particular, the Employment Opportunity Pilot Project (EOPP) surveys, the Small Business Administration (SBA) surveys, a survey financed by the W.E. Upjohn Institute, and a unique company-specific database compiled by Bartel (1995) have provided new opportunities for analyzing the decision-making process and outcomes with regard to education and training from the employers' perspective. And the National Longitudinal Survey (NLS) and Current Population Survey (CPS) provide information for analyzing the receipt of training from the workers' perspective, including its impact on wages.

The studies of Barron, Berger, and Black (1999) and Loewenstein and Spletzer (1998, 1999) provide the following insights:

- The theoretical distinction between general and firm-specific training seems in reality to be highly blurred. Much education or training that is provided and financed by employers does, indeed, appear to be "general." Moreover, there is little evidence to suggest that employees "pay for" general education through wage reductions (as is suggested by human capital theory in its purest form).

- Employers experience the benefits of productivity gains that result from their investments in both general and firm-specific training, and can recoup the costs of those investments.

- Similarly, employees who receive either general or firm-specific training enjoy higher wages as a result of those employer-financed benefits (although the wage benefits of general training appear to manifest themselves more in higher wages at subsequent jobs, rather than in the form of higher wages with their current employer). (Also see Bartel 1995.)

Barron, Berger, and Black's 1997 analysis demonstrates that, despite improvements in measuring workplace education and training, considerable measurement error remains. They note that such measurement error is likely to lead to a significant underestimation of the benefits of workplace education, both to employers and employees. Despite such potential for underestimation, the benefits (in the form of both higher productivity and higher wages) are seen to be substantial (see, for example, Mincer's 1989 review of the literature, as well as the more recent literature already cited). In fact, the benefits substantially exceed "normal" rates of return, strongly suggesting that the market may fail to produce the socially optimal level of workplace education and training.

In short, the recent literature provides ample evidence that the operation of the labor market is considerably less "perfect" than that required for Becker's predictions to hold on a universal basis. Employers do provide and finance general training. And although both employers and employees benefit from this provision, there is reason to believe (given the above-normal rates of return) that the level of training is suboptimal. The literature is, however, almost completely silent on the issue of potential market failure, as well as on two important and related issues: first, the implications of these labor market "imperfections" for lower-wage workers, and second, the public policy implications of these findings.

We explore these questions, among others, in the research initiative described in the following chapters. Chapter 2 provides some definitions and briefly describes the three phases of the multipart research effort. Chapter 3 discusses phase 1, the analysis of quantitative data contained in a unique database collected by the American Society for Training and Development (ASTD). Chapter 4 explores information of a more qualitative nature, gathered through phase 2, telephone surveys of employers who provide training to lower-wage workers. The next six chapters (5 through 10) discuss phase 3, seven individual case studies of organizations with particularly notable programs for lower-wage worker training (two of the organizations from the health care industry are described in a single chapter; each of the other organizations is covered in a separate chapter). Chapter 11 summarizes the lessons learned from the case studies. Chapter 12 draws some conclusions and discusses the policy implications of our research.

2
Methods

In three distinct but related phases of research, this project examines the questions described in the previous chapter: How much training is provided to lower-wage workers? Who tends to provide it? What barriers are there to effective training and what enables it? What roles do supply and demand play in determining how much training is provided? And what role might external incentives play?

THE THREE PHASES OF THE RESEARCH

In the first phase we ran a statistical analysis on the database on employers' workplace education and training practices created by the American Society for Training and Development (ASTD) (see Chapter 3). We used this database to analyze the attributes that distinguish employers who make unusually high investments (in terms of amount, content, or effectiveness) in education and training for lower-wage workers. This analysis generated, first, empirical insights into some of the factors that contribute to the generally low levels of workplace training that prevail for lower-wage workers, and second, a profile of 192 employers that we identified as investing most heavily in training for lower-wage workers. We describe the results of phase 1 in Chapter 3.

We then used this profile of the 192 employers from phase 1 to identify a further group of 40 employers who served as the foundation for the second phase of the study. For each of these 40 organizations the empirical analysis of phase 1 had shown evidence of some form of unusual or above-average commitment to providing training for their lower-wage workers. We conducted structured telephone interviews with these 40 employers to learn more about the forces behind their education and training strategies, the impact of those strategies, and the barriers that the organizations faced in making training available to lower-wage workers. We discuss these results in Chapter 4.

Finally, we used the results of the telephone surveys as the foundation for the third phase of the study—site visits and case studies of eight of the 40 employers we had interviewed by telephone in the second phase. Our primary consideration in identifying organizations for case studies was a qualitative assessment of the extent to which the telephone survey information showed them to be making extraordinarily high investments in education and training for lower-wage workers (again, in terms of amount, content, or effectiveness). This phase of the study generated a rich qualitative understanding of the organizations' motivations, successes, and barriers, as well as of the perspectives of lower-wage workers themselves. We discuss these results in Chapters 5 to 11.

DEFINITION OF WORKERS AT RISK

This study was designed to focus on workplace education and training for those individuals who are in the greatest jeopardy of experiencing declining wages or job loss as a result of rapid and fundamental changes in the economy. Ideally, therefore, such a study would have specifically examined those workers who have the fewest marketable skills. Unfortunately, no standard, widely used definitions or measurements of skill are available. This is particularly evident in the aggregate data from the employers who were the main source of empirical information for this study. The best available proxy variables were wage levels and (when available) education levels. Hence, much of the analysis and discussion that follows focuses on "lower-wage" workers.

Even for these variables, however, there is no clear line that enables us to easily identify workers of interest. In consultation with the advisory board for this research initiative, we agreed upon a necessarily imperfect working definition for identifying at-risk workers: The research would focus on "lower-wage workers," defined as "those workers (in the United States) earning $10 per hour or less."

As mentioned earlier, the heterogeneity of the lower-wage population also represents a significant analytic problem, since some individuals in this group do not share the same "at risk" qualities. Nevertheless, we are reasonably satisfied that workers in this category as a whole are far more representative of the population at risk than any other group that could be defined given data constraints. When possible, parts of the analysis also consider education level (in particular, a high school education or less) as a factor in most accurately identifying the group of at-risk workers being studied.

It should be noted that during the period in which we were conducting our research (late 1999 through summer 2000), the United States was experiencing historically low rates of unemployment, resulting in an uncharacteristically tight labor market. Many of the employers with whom we had contact mentioned this factor as a primary consideration in shaping their training strategy. As this book went to press, the unemployment rate had risen significantly, but we have retained the mentions of the labor market conditions as they existed during our research.

QUANTITATIVE DATA: THE ASTD DATABASE

The primary source of quantitative data for this study was a major initiative that had been launched by ASTD in 1997, the ASTD Benchmarking Service. This initiative gathers a wide variety of data on employers' education and training investments and practices. ASTD continues to operate this service at the time of publication. Through the benchmarking service, employers submit data to ASTD on their formal training investments, using a common set of definitions and metrics. ASTD then returns to the employers a customized benchmarking report that enables them to compare their investments with those of other (comparable) employers. This process generates a large database that can be used for a variety of research purposes. At first most of the questions in the database related to organizations as a whole, without any effort to identify practices for lower-wage employees. ASTD did, however, include a few questions focused on lower-wage workers, in the hope of learning more about the incidence and effectiveness of such training.

In 1998, ASTD expanded its service in two significant ways: first, to collect standard ("benchmarkable") data on the *outcomes* of employers' education and training practices, and second, to collect additional data on education investments and outcomes for lower-wage workers. The content of the data collected has remained relatively similar in subsequent years. At the time of writing, the research database contains employer-level information on formal education and training investments and practices for approximately 2,500 employers (about two-thirds of which are U.S. based) and summary information on "learning outcomes" from over 300,000 individual assessments from approximately 230 employers. The database that was available for the analyses in this book included the U.S.-based 1997 and 1998[1] data gathered through the ASTD *Measurement Kit* (ASTD 1997, 1998), the actual ASTD data collection instrument. The training investment data for 1997 include the responses of 754 organizations, and for 1998, 546 organizations. The database for 1999 and 2000 was not yet available and those data are not, therefore, included here.

ASTD accepts training data from any organization interested in providing them in exchange for benchmarking comparisons. As a result, the database is not a random sample of firms and does not necessarily represent the population as a whole. Nevertheless, comparisons of the first year of ASTD data with a random sample of employer data that had been gathered some years earlier by the Bureau of Labor Statistics (BLS) show that the general characteristics of the firms in the ASTD database are quite similar to those of the firms in the random BLS sample. This finding gives us confidence that we may reasonably draw quantitative conclusions from the ASTD data on some matters (as in Chapter 3) and cautiously apply them to the population as a whole.[2]

QUALITATIVE DATA

Beyond our initial quantitative data analysis, our research depended on other sources of information. In particular, in phases 2 and 3, we made extensive use of qualitative data-gathering techniques, which allowed us to consider the results from the ASTD data in light of information gained through a different perspective.

Telephone Surveys

In an effort to gather additional, qualitative information on employers' training practices for lower-wage employees (beyond the small amount of data specific to lower-wage and other at-risk workers that were already collected in the ASTD database), we conducted 40 telephone surveys with selected employers. Because a primary question in this research is whether such training is effective in the small number of organizations that make an extensive commitment to it, and what specific barriers or enablers those firms encountered in their experience with training lower-wage workers, we decided to focus the telephone surveys on only those employers that provided more lower-wage worker training (either total or per worker) than the average firm.

All but two of these employers were included in a group of firms identified as "lower-wage training intensive" (LWTI) in the analysis of the quantitative ASTD data. These firms make a greater-than-average commitment to training lower-wage workers, either because they give more training per lower-wage worker or because a larger percentage of the workforce falls into the lower-wage category. We describe the group of firms included in the telephone surveys, and the methods we used to identify them, in more detail in Chapter 4. In addition, using alternative methods, including published articles and contacts from our research initiative advisory board, we identified and included two organizations outside the ASTD database with reputations for a strong commitment to lower-wage worker training.

We contacted the selected organizations and asked them to participate in a 20- to 30-minute telephone survey (see Appendix A for the full slate of questions). The questions covered a wide range of issues related to lower-wage worker training, including the following:

- the percentage of lower-wage workers in the organization,
- the typical positions of lower-wage workers,
- any change over time in the representation of such workers in the workforce,
- the types of training provided (content) to lower-wage workers,
- the methods of providing or delivering that training,
- the primary benefits of such training,

- the departmental responsibilities for training lower-wage workers,

- any barriers they identified to making such training effective, and conversely,

- any enablers that increased its effectiveness.

To encourage candid responses, we promised participating organizations that their responses could be kept anonymous. The results of these telephone surveys, as discussed in Chapter 4, provide a more detailed picture of training for lower-wage workers inside firms that conduct such training on a greater-than-average basis.[3]

Case Studies

Finally, in the third phase of the research, we conducted case studies of seven employers (including site visits) in an effort to learn more about the organizations that the second research phase (the telephone surveys) had identified as making an extremely significant commitment in at least some aspect of providing training opportunities to lower-wage workers.[4] We selected organizations for the case studies because they appeared to be enjoying unusual success in their training for lower-wage workers or because they appeared to be providing more (or a broader range) of training opportunities for lower-wage workers than even the average LWTI organization.

To identify the candidate organizations for inclusion in the case studies we evaluated their responses to the telephone survey described above. We scored each respondent on a relative scale of 1 to 5 on each of the 10 "key themes" that emerged from the telephone surveys. (Table 4.3 in Chapter 4 identifies these themes.) Organizations received higher scores for more extensive, more broadly developed, or more promising practices and experiences for a given theme. Organizations with the highest total scores became candidates for case-study analysis. In choosing the final list of case-study candidates, we took into account some demographic factors, such as firm size, industry, and geographic location, in an effort to draw a more diverse group of firms for the case studies. Table 2.1 lists the organizations that we included in the case studies along with general information on each organization's location, industry, and number of employees.

Table 2.1 Organizations Included in Case-Study Site Visits

Organization	Location	Industry	Number of employees[a]
Boeing Employees' Credit Union	Tukwila, WA	Financial services	850
CVS	Woonsocket, RI	Retail: chain drug stores	100,000
Lacks Enterprises	Grand Rapids, MI	Manufacturing	1,800
LYNX	Orlando, FL	Public transit	480
Mary Greeley Medical Center	Ames, IA	Health care	1,400
UPMC-Passavant	Pittsburgh, PA	Health care	1,500
Wyoming Student Loan Corporation	Cheyenne, WY	Financial services	46

[a] Approximate, as reported by the organization in the summer of 2000.
SOURCE: Information gathered by authors through telephone interviews and site visits.

Having determined the list of organizations for case study, we contacted the organizations for permission to visit. During the initial contacts, we informed the organizations that each would be asked to 1) review the written report of our visit (essentially the individual chapter written about each company later in this book), 2) correct any factual errors, and 3) then choose whether the organization's identity should remain anonymous when the results were made public. (In the end, all participating firms agreed to have their identities included in the final report.)

Because of the small size of our sample, the organizations we studied may not be representative of the population of organizations that provide unusual training opportunities to lower-wage workers. A number of potentially important factors were not considered in selecting firms. As a result, the effect of unions, for example, was not a factor in the training efforts at any of our case-study organizations. Most notably, the majority of the organizations are not-for-profits, a point we discuss in additional detail later in the book. Nevertheless, we strongly believe that the organizations we studied provide important and helpful insights about the hows and whys of providing training to lower-wage workers.

In the summer of 2000 we made site visits to the seven different organizations that met the necessary criteria. Each site visit was conducted by a team of two of the three authors (with the composition of the teams rotating). Each visit included discussions with management and training staff, tours of the premises, and interviews with lower-wage employees (usually on an individual basis, always in the absence of representatives of management). The employees interviewed were identified by management. We requested that they select a group of employees who would provide us with significant diversity in the areas of job tenure, department or position within the organization, and extent of training participation (if applicable).

We discussed the following points with management:

- the nature of training offered (content, delivery methods, and whether it was voluntary or mandatory);

- the primary motivation for the types of training available to lower-wage workers;

- the specific barriers and enablers encountered in providing training for lower-wage workers;

- the primary benefits or drawbacks of such training; and

- the overall organizational philosophy regarding training for lower-wage workers.

We discussed the following points with individual lower-wage workers:

- the nature of training offered (content, delivery methods, and whether voluntary or mandatory);

- how much training they received;

- whether available training met their needs;

- what other types of training they would like to have available.

Appendix B shows the full template of questions and issues covered in the case-study visits.

The case studies thus allowed us to make more detailed observations and draw finer conclusions than either of the previous phases of our research. For example, they included the only firsthand perspectives from lower-wage workers themselves regarding issues related to the training opportunities that they received or wished to receive. In addition, most of the case studies provided a higher-level perspective from within the organization's management structure, which enabled us to gain a better understanding of the organizational and strategic context in which firms with a strong commitment to lower-wage worker training viewed that training.

We discuss the results of the seven case studies in Chapters 5 through 10 (two organizations in the same industry are combined into one chapter), and in Chapter 11 we summarize the lessons we learned from them.

SOME CAVEATS

The results of each of the three complementary phases of the research analysis are described in additional detail in the following chapters. It is worth noting that, while the second and third phases of the research study provided more detailed information as well as rich insights into specific practices and perspectives related to lower-wage worker training, this analysis is by no means representative. For example, we would expect that, on average, trainers, employees, and staff would be likely to be overly positive or optimistic in their comments to researchers on their training initiatives and offerings. Moreover, we had selected the organizations included in the analysis precisely because of their unusual focus on training for lower-wage workers. Throughout our research and analysis, we have made significant efforts to compensate for these biases when possible, both in the questions we asked and, when necessary, in describing the results. But in the end, our research is—by design—an examination of a highly unusual phenomenon, and should be interpreted as such.

Notes

1. We adjusted the 1997 financial data for inflation so they would be comparable to the 1998 data.
2. Although we cannot definitely determine the representativeness (or lack thereof) of the ASTD database, we believe that the issue is, fortunately, largely irrelevant for the primary questions in our research. We focus on distinguishing among employers on two dimensions: 1) the degree to which they appear to provide training to lower-wage workers, and 2) the distinguishing attributes of employers that do and do not provide substantial amounts of such training. There

is little reason to believe that our ability to distinguish among employers on these two fronts would be affected by any potential nonrandomness (in terms of the overall incidence or intensity of training) of those organizations that choose to report their data to ASTD.

3. A few participating organizations asked to remain anonymous. The remaining participants were: Agilent Technologies; Alcon Laboratories/Fort Worth Manufacturing; Boeing Employees' Credit Union; Bridge Community Support Services Training Network; California Christian Hospital/National Benevolent Association; City of Lubbock; Country Meadows; Diamond Products; Digital Graphics Advantage; Fazoli's Restaurant; Flying J, Inc.; Furr's Restaurant Group, Inc.; Holiday Inn Research Park; Intersil; Lane Press; Lemforder Corp.; Long Beach Transit; Lucent Technologies/Cirent Semiconductor; LYNX—Central Florida Regional Transportation Authority; Mary Greeley Medical Center; Northwest Missouri Psychiatric Rehabilitation Center; Parkview Health System–Parkview Hospital; Purdue University Libraries; Sarah Bush Lincoln Health Center; ServiceMaster Co. Management Services; Stuller Companies; Texas A & M University; Uno Restaurant Corp.; UPMC-Passavant; Van Kampen Investments; Walgreen's; Woodhaven Learning Center/National Benevolent Association; and Yuasa, Inc.

4. We conducted an eighth case study as well, but omitted it from the discussion in this book because the visit revealed that the organization did not meet the standard of being significantly ahead of others in terms of the training opportunities they provide to lower-wage workers.

3
Phase 1
Analysis of ASTD Data

This chapter provides a brief statistical overview, based on all the available information in the 1997 and 1998 ASTD databases (covering a total of 1,300 firms) of employers' training practices for lower-wage workers. It focuses primarily on the 192 organizations that we identified as providing unusual amounts of education and training to their lower-wage workers, measured using both expenditures and time devoted to formal training. (No reliable data are available on informal training).[1]

The questions relevant to lower-wage workers changed from 1997 to 1998. In 1998, employers were asked what percentage of their total training expenditures went toward the training of employees with fewer than 12 years of education. Of those that responded to this question, 47 percent reported that they spent nothing training this group, and only 10 percent reported spending 15 percent or more of their total training expenditures on this group. Follow-up telephone surveys (to verify the responses of all those who had reported a percentage other than zero to this question) revealed that: 1) many respondents do not hire people with less than a high school education, 2) many are not able to accurately separate this group out from those who have a high school education but no more, and 3) some respondents misinterpreted this question and responded with data for people who have more than a high school education.[2]

The questions for the 1997 data had been somewhat different. The respondents were asked what percentage of their workforce earned less than $10 per hour, as well as what percentage had less than a high school education. Respondents were also asked what percentage of workers in each group received training. The results for 1997 were as follows:

- Regarding the wage: nearly 20 percent of the respondents reported employing no one earning less than $10 per hour; 50 percent of the respondents employed at least 10 percent of their employees at $10 per hour; and 15 percent of the respondents reported that at least 50 percent of their workforce earned less than $10 per hour.

• Regarding high school education: 50 percent of the 1997 sample reported that 1 percent or fewer of their employees lacked high school diplomas; only 2 percent of the respondents reported that 50 percent or more of their workforce lacked high school diplomas.

• Regarding training: Employers provided training to workers in the lower-wage and less-educated categories, but at somewhat lower levels than to employees who did not fall into those groups. According to ASTD, the mean firm in its database provided training to 74 percent of its workers (Bassi and Van Buren 1999). About 50 percent of the organizations that employed people at wages of less than $10 per hour provided training to at least 75 percent of such workers, while only about 40 percent of employers provided training to at least 75 percent of their employees who lacked high school diplomas. The remaining organizations provided training to less than 75 percent of their employees in these lower-wage and less-educated groups.

In both years, identical questions were asked about organizations' training expenditures on basic skills courses (which is one of 13 different content categories included in the survey, and the only one likely to pertain primarily to lower-wage workers). Only 25 percent of organizations spent 1 percent or more of their training budgets on basic skills training courses, and only 8 percent of the total sample spent 5 percent or more of that budget on basic skills courses.

LOWER-WAGE TRAINING INTENSIVE (LWTI) FIRMS

We needed to find out what types of organizations devoted disproportionate resources to training for lower-wage workers. By combining the variables related to lower-wage workers from the 1998 and 1997 data, we identified those organizations that seemed to be devoting the most resources to training lower-wage workers and flagged them as "lower-wage training intensive" (LWTI) firms.[3] The data show that firms could fall into this group for either of two main reasons. First, they might have a larger percentage of lower-wage workers than other firms (and also provide at least some training to those workers, although not necessarily a large amount of training per worker). Or, relative to the average firm, they might provide a disproportionately high amount of per capita training to their lower-wage workers (although their percentage of lower-wage workers might still be quite low).

We found that the LWTI organizations represent 15 percent of the sample, or 192 organizations. Table 3.1 compares the LWTI organizations with the overall sample in terms of organizational statistics. As the table shows, higher concentrations of LWTI organizations are found in health care than in other industries, while finance, insurance, and real estate companies, as well as technology companies, are underrepresented in the LWTI group. The sample's highest representation of LWTI organizations is disproportionately found in the midwest. Publicly traded and for-profit organizations are less likely to be deemed LWTI than their counterparts, and LWTI organizations are disproportionately likely to be family-owned.

PATTERNS IN KEY TRAINING MEASURES

The ASTD database provides a set of "key training ratios"—eight different measures for capturing the extent of an organization's training investments. These key ratios represent another prism through which LWTI organizations can be viewed relative to the overall sample. Table 3.2 lists these key ratios and compares the mean values found for LWTI organizations with those found for other organizations.

Somewhat surprisingly, LWTI organizations spend less per employee on training than other organizations ($557 per employee in LWTI organizations versus $763 per employee in other organizations), as well as less on training as a percentage of payroll. At the same time, however, the percentage of employees trained in LWTI organizations is actually greater than in other organizations, as is the number of train-

Table 3.1 Characteristics of LWTI Organizations Compared with Overall Sample, Percent Composition

Organizations by group	LWTI organizations	Overall sample
Grouped by size		
1–499 employees	**34.9**	**38.3**
500–1,999 employees	**37.5**	**31.1**
2,000+ employees	27.6	30.6
Grouped by industry		
Agriculture, mining, construction	**0.5**	**1.8**
Trade	7.2	5.9
Government	6.7	8.1
Finance, insurance, real estate	**8.8**	**16.5**
Durables	10.8	10.0
Nondurables	10.3	9.0
Technology	**11.9**	**15.8**
Health care	**20.1**	**7.0**
Services	16.0	16.4
Transportation, public utilities	7.7	8.3
Grouped by U.S. region		
Northeast	17.0	17.8
South	28.9	30.7
Midwest	**35.6**	**30.9**
West	18.6	20.6
For-profit	**58.6**	**67.0**
Family owned	**16.2**	**12.2**
Publicly traded	**30.9**	**40.0**

NOTE: Overall sample size—1,300 organizations (including 192 LWTI companies). Bold type denotes significant difference between means at 0.05 level.
SOURCE: Authors' analysis of survey data and information from ASTD 1997 and 1998 "Part I" data (submitted in 1998 and 1999).

ing hours per employee (89 percent and 71 percent, respectively), although the latter difference is not statistically significant. Several factors may explain these results:

• The mean LWTI organization is typically smaller, in terms of both payroll and number of employees, than other organizations (see Table 3.3), and smaller organizations typically spend less on training.

Table 3.2   Comparison of Mean Values of Key Training Ratios for LWTI and Other Organizations

	Mean values	
Key training ratios	LWIT organizations	Other organizations
Total training expenditures per employee, dollars	**$557.09**	**$762.81**
Total training expenditures as a percentage of payroll	**1.61%**	**2.05%**
Percent of employees trained	**88.67%**	**71.45%**
Employee-to-trainer ratio	382 to 1	374 to 1
Percent of training time via classroom instruction	**74.33%**	**78.62%**
Percent of training time via learning technologies	9.21%	8.98%
Payments to outside companies as a percentage of expenditures	23.02%	26.36%
Number of training hours per employee	34.10	27.16

NOTE: Overall sample size—1,300 organizations (including 192 LWTI companies). Bold type denotes significant difference between means at 0.05 level.
SOURCE: Authors' analysis of survey data and information from ASTD 1997 and 1998 "Part I" data (submitted in 1998 and 1999).

- LWTI organizations rely less on classroom delivery (and more on other delivery methods, including the use of electronic learning technology, which is often less expensive per worker).

- The content of training most commonly provided to lower-wage workers (for example, orientation and safety) is likely to be less expensive than that provided to higher-wage workers (leadership and professional skills development).

Table 3.3 compares various organizational and training measures found in LWTI organizations with those in other organizations, showing mean values for each. The table provides additional insight into the traits and training practices that differentiate LWTI organizations from others. Although correlations do not necessarily prove a causal relationship, they do suggest some interesting possibilities in this case.[4] The positive relationship between the percentage of employees receiving training and LWTI organizations, for example, suggests that LWTI organizations are more concerned about training *all* their employees, and that the training opportunities provided by these organizations to their lower-wage employees likely reflect in many ways the opportunities provided to their entire workforce. Consistent with this possibility,

Table 3.3 Comparison of Mean Values of Organization and Training Measures for LWTI and Other Organizations

Variable	Mean values	
	LWTI organizations	Other organizations
Number of employees	3,590	6,392
Payroll (millions)	$131	$236
% of training expenditures on new employee orientation	9.8	7.1
% of training expenditures on sales and dealer training	4.1	6.1
% of training expenditures on information technology skills	10.0	12.5
% of IT training expenditures on administrative employees	25.5	16.0
% of IT training expenditures on sales employees	1.3	5.4
% of employees who received training last year	84.7	65.4
% of employees who will receive training next year	90.3	79.9
Use of 4-year colleges/universities to deliver training	14.5	27.7
Use of product suppliers to deliver training	75.3	62.6
Use of federal, state, or local government organizations to deliver training	31.2	22.5
Use of cable television to distribute training	11.7	6.0
Use of intranet to distribute training	20.7	29.4
Use of local area networks (LAN) to distribute training	28.3	35.9
Use of annual performance reviews	99.5	97.5
Use of skill certification	80.1	69.7
Use of teleconferencing to present training	41.7	30.0
Use of mandatory annual training time	68.6	49.6
Use of line-on-loan or rotational training staff	23.3	30.4
Use of job rotation or cross-training	92.7	86.0
Use of total quality management (TQM) diagnostics	78.6	72.1

NOTE: Overall sample size—1,300 organizations (including 192 LWTI companies). *All* findings included in this table are statistically significant at the 0.05 level.
SOURCE: Authors' analysis of survey data and information from ASTD 1997 and 1998 "Part I" data (submitted in 1998 and 1999).

LWTI organizations spend a larger percentage of their training expenditures on new-employee orientation, suggesting that such organizations may perhaps provide new-employee orientation broadly, to almost all their employees, regardless of their job positions or titles. It is also not surprising to see that mandatory training is correlated with the training of lower-wage employees. The results of the telephone survey (discussed in Chapter 4) support these two findings, as many respondents mentioned orientation and mandatory courses required by regulation as common types of training that they provide to their lower-wage employees. The telephone surveys also support the correlation between LWTI organizations and their rating on their ability to retain employees. Over half the telephone survey respondents mentioned that they used training of lower-wage employees as a recruitment and retention tool.

Other notable statistically significant correlation differences include information technology (IT) training practices. LWTI firms spend a smaller percentage of their total training expenditures on IT training, but spend a much *higher* percentage of those IT expenditures on employees at the administrative level (26 percent of IT expenditures, versus 16 percent for non-LWTI firms), again consistent with the observation that such firms may tend to spread training more broadly through the organization, even in uncommon areas. LWTI firms are less likely to use computer-based technology, such as intranets and local area networks (LANs), to provide training. Fewer LWTI firms use universities or four-year colleges as providers of training, but more of them use product suppliers, or training provided by government organizations at the federal, state, or local level. Overall, the quantitative results point to clear bands of differences in training practices between LWTI firms and non-LWTI firms. We examine the nature of the average LWTI firm's perspective in additional detail in the coming chapters.

THE IMPACT OF EMPLOYER-PROVIDED TRAINING

Part II of the ASTD *Measurement Kit* is designed to provide "benchmarkable" measures of the learning outcomes that result from training.[5] Three different measurements are used to capture these outcomes. The first (the initial evaluation) is roughly akin to Kirkpatrick's level 1 evaluation (Kirkpatrick 1998).[6] It measures learners' assessments of the potential *utility* of what they have learned.[7] The second and third measures are follow-up evaluations, similar to Kirkpatrick's level 3 evaluation. One of these focuses on learners' assessments of the productivity effects of the learning intervention at some point (typically three to six months after the intervention), and the other focuses on supervisors' assessments of the same productivity effects.

Respondents to Part II of ASTD's *Measurement Kit* provided background information regarding their lower-wage population. They were asked

- if most employees in their courses had completed fewer than 12 years of formal education (1998 and 1997 data), and

- if most employees in those courses earned $10 an hour or less (1997 data only).

For the purposes of analyzing the outcomes data, an answer of "yes" to either question earned the course a "lower-wage-oriented" flag. Just under 10 percent of the 831 course types for which data were submitted were given this designation. Although it is possible that many of the participants in some of these classes did not fall into the at-risk category, it is still true that more of the recipients were lower-wage in those classes than in the other 90 percent of the courses for which data were submitted.

Participants in courses oriented toward the lower-wage group *initially* reacted less favorably to their courses (that is, they assessed the courses' potential utility lower) than did participants in courses not made up primarily of lower-wage coworkers.[8] Their average follow-up evaluation, however (assessing the courses' productivity effect), was more favorable than that of those in courses not oriented toward lower-wage participants. (These differences in *follow-up* results were not, however, statistically significant.) Table 3.4 shows participants' initial and follow-up responses to the course evaluation.

Table 3.5 displays supervisors' assessments of how their employees' performance changed as a result of the courses they took. These results indicate that supervisors also assessed the longer-term impacts of lower-wage-oriented courses as being greater than those for courses

Table 3.4 Comparison of Participants' Initial and Follow-Up Evaluations of Lower-Wage-Oriented Courses and Other Courses

Participant evaluation questions	Lower-wage-oriented courses	Other courses
	Average ranking by participants[a]	
Initial evaluation		
"My knowledge and/or skills increased as a result of this course."	*3.89*	*4.28*
"The knowledge and/or skills gained through this course are directly applicable to my job."	*3.97*	*4.30*
	Average value of x given by participants, percent	
Follow-up evaluation		
"As a result of this course, my performance on the course objectives has changed by x percent."	34.5	21.2
"As a result of this course, my overall job performance has changed by x percent."	30.4	20.1

[a] Participants answered the initial evaluation questions using a 5-point scale, with 1 = "strongly disagree" and 5 = "strongly agree."

NOTE: Overall sample size: 262 organizations; 1,581 composite "course-category" submissions, 12,060 separate courses, 400,000 individual assessments of learning outcomes. (Respondents were asked to combine all responses for similar types of courses into a single data submission. Thus 10 "basic skills" courses would all be reported as one composite course-category submission; similarly, 15 "interpersonal skills" courses would be combined and reported as another composite data submission.) Numbers in bold italics are significant at the 0.05 level.

SOURCE Authors' analysis of survey data and information from ASTD 1997 and 1998 "Part II" data (submitted in 1998 and 1999).

Table 3.5 Comparison of Supervisors' Follow-Up Evaluations of Employees' Performance after Receipt of Training

Follow-up evaluation	Score (x), percent	
	Lower-wage-oriented courses	Other courses
"As a result of this course, his/her performance on the course objectives has changed by x percent."	24.4	20.1
"As a result of this course, his/her overall job performance has changed by x percent."	30.8	19.1

NOTE: Overall sample size: 262 organizations; 1,581 composite "course-category" submissions, 12,060 separate courses, 400,000 individual assessments of learning outcomes.

SOURCE: Authors' analysis of survey data and information from ASTD 1997 and 1998 "Part II" data (submitted in 1998 and 1999).

that were not oriented primarily to lower-wage/lower-education employees (although again these results are not statistically significant).

Since level 1 evaluations are the most commonly used type of evaluation (especially in comparison with level 3 evaluations), it is possible that organizations finding less than desirable results through level 1 evaluations of courses oriented to lower-wage workers have, therefore, chosen to direct more of their resources toward training other groups of employees. The results summarized above suggest that, unless they wait to gather follow-up information, organizations' decisions on whether or not to train their employees may not be valid if they are based only on initial participant reaction.

SUMMARY OF FINDINGS

Organizations that provide an above-average level of training for their lower-wage employees are likely to have between 500 and 2,000 employees. Health care and family-owned, not-for-profit, and privately held organizations also tend to provide more training to lower-wage employees than other organizations. They tend to spend less than other organizations, however, on training per employee and as a percentage of payroll even though they generally train a higher percentage of their employees overall. They also tend to rely somewhat less on classroom training, to dedicate slightly more resources to new-employee orientation, and to be more likely to use government sources to deliver training than other organizations.

In terms of learning outcomes, courses composed primarily of lower-wage employees are not evaluated favorably by participants immediately following their completion. However, after time has passed, participants and their supervisors assess the productivity effects of courses provided primarily to lower-wage workers as being greater than those of courses provided primarily to higher-wage employees.

Notes

1. One possibility, of course, is that training of lower-wage workers is primarily informal in nature, and therefore is not reflected in data on formal training expenditures. Unfortunately, we do not have the necessary data to examine this possibility.

2. Using other available measures, we were able to screen the data for internal consistency and thereby eliminate organizations that appeared to have misinterpreted the relevant question.

3. We identified an organization as LWTI if it ranked above a certain threshold on any one of three different measures. First, from the 1998 data, we flagged as LWTI all organizations reporting that 15 percent or more of their training expenditures went toward lower-wage workers. Second, for the 1997 data, we first ranked the "percentage receiving training" variables of both those employees earning less than $10 an hour and those who had less than a high school education. We then examined the distribution of the rankings and flagged the top 25 percent of the organizations training high percentages of employees with lower wages and less than a high school education. Finally, we pooled the data from 1998 and 1997 and chose those organizations whose expenditures on basic skills training fell into the top 10 percent of the total distribution.

4. In addition to the descriptive statistics summarized in Tables 3.1 to 3.3, we ran numerous linear and logit regression models. None of those models, however, sheds any light on the factors affecting the likelihood that an organization is LWTI in its practice of training lower-wage employees.

5. ASTD's purpose in making the *Measurement Kit* available is to present a way to benchmark both learning processes and learning outcomes so that enterprises can assess when their results fall inside or outside of acceptable ranges. The *Measurement Kit* enables enterprises to measure their learning outcomes against these benchmarks at two different stages: 1) an initial evaluation, which can be administered to learners at the conclusion of the learning event; and 2) a follow-up evaluation, which can be administered to learners and their supervisors from three to 12 months after the learning event ends.

6. In the 1950s, Donald Kirkpatrick proposed a four-level system for evaluating the outcomes that result from education and training: level 1—student reaction, level 2—student learning, level 3—transfer of learning to the job, and level 4—business results. After Kirkpatrick's original work, other authors proposed a fifth level—return on investment (ROI). The most updated version of the evaluation system he began in the 1950s is described in Kirkpatrick 1998.

7. Thus, it is somewhat different from the more traditional "smile sheet" level 1 assessment.

8. One possible explanation for these differences is that they result from a "composition effect" (that is, if lower-wage workers are disproportionately likely to be taking courses that typically receive low initial evaluations but higher follow-up evaluations). Regression results, however, did not support this explanation. In

fact, even after controlling for course type, a course's LWTI designation has a statistically significant negative effect on participants' initial evaluations of the course. Regression results with respect to both participants' and supervisors' follow-up evaluations are inconclusive with respect to controlling for course type.

4
Phase 2
Results of the Telephone Surveys

As we summarized the results of phase 2—the telephone surveys we conducted with the 40 organizations we found to be making above-average investments in training for lower-wage workers—several broad themes emerged: We found that we could classify the organizations on the basis of their training motivations; we were able to compare the details of the training provided; we noted the barriers to such training as well as some things that appeared to enable the training; and we assessed the impact of the training. We discuss these themes in this chapter.

CLASSIFICATIONS BASED ON TRAINING MOTIVATION

Most fundamentally, we found that throughout the training programs discussed in the surveys, the needs of the organization typically superseded those of individual employees. Thus, as one would expect, employers provided training for lower-wage employees, not simply to "do good," but because it is good for business. Three separate factors emerged as the primary motivation for the provision of such training. These factors underscore significant differences among the firms in various other training-related areas as well.

In some cases, market forces represented the primary motivation behind an organization's decision to provide training. In others, the organization's particular line of business, coupled with regulatory and other external requirements, made training necessary. Most (approximately 80 percent) of the organizations included in the telephone surveys fell into one of these two categories; in both categories, economic factors are the primary motivation behind training.

For the remaining 20 percent of organizations, although economic factors were also important, they were not the only major force driving their training strategy. Such firms appear to be particularly friendly to lower-wage workers. They tend to operate under the philosophy that providing training to all employees—especially voluntary training—benefits not only the organization (in terms of profits, productivity, and employee retention), but also the employees' skills, morale, work-life balance, and belief in their opportunities to advance within the organization. We might categorize such organizations as believing that "doing good" and pursuing good business practices are wholly complementary. They focus heavily on the needs of their employees, therefore, confident in the belief that most actions in that pursuit will also advance their business goals.

On the basis of these observations, we classified each of the participating 40 organizations into one of three different motivation-oriented categories, with additional typical characteristics as described below:[1]

1) *Philosophy-driven organizations:* Training and development in these firms have historically been part of the firm's organizational cultures and are believed to play strategic roles in increasing their flexibility, employee retention, and the quality of services or products. These firms have a commitment to training that stems from factors as much cultural as economic. They represent a relatively small number of the organizations surveyed.

2) *Market-driven organizations:* Training strategies in these firms are shaped primarily by economic factors, including the level of unemployment, the level of education of the workforce, the industry's growth, and increases in customer service expectations. The key characteristics of their training programs are strongly linked to external environmental factors, including industry standards, the level of unemployment, the level of education of the labor market, and the profitability of the sector.

3) *Nature-of-work-driven organizations:* Training strategies in these firms have evolved gradually through time with the goal of better leveraging of human resources in often highly specialized industries. As with market-driven organizations, the key characteristics of their training programs are strongly linked to external environmental factors.

Table 4.1 describes the demographic characteristics of the firms in the study, broken down by motivation group.

Table 4.1 Distribution of Organizations by Motivation Group

	Philosophy driven	Market driven	Nature-of-work driven
Number of organizations	8	16	16
Average number of employees	2,747	43,102	1,840
	Number of respondents		
Size distribution			
1–499	3	4	6
500–1,999	3	6	7
2,000+	2	6	3
Industry distribution			
Trade	1	4	0
Government	1	1	0
Finance, insurance, real estate	1	1	1
Durables	0	2	2
Nondurables	0	0	3
Technology	0	0	3
Health care	2	2	3
Services	3	3	3
Transportation/public utilities	0	3	1

SOURCE: Authors' analysis of survey data and information from ASTD Benchmarking Database 1997 and 1998 "Part I" data (submitted in 1998 and 1999).

We can also identify 10 key themes that organizations consistently must address when they provide training. Table 4.2 defines these themes in the form of the questions that the organizations were required to answer in our survey. Each of the three types of organizations reacts to these themes differently; Table 4.3 depicts a matrix of the common reactions or responses to the 10 themes, broken down by motivational group. It is important to note that not all behaviors are necessarily pursued by all the firms in a given group. These themes are discussed in additional detail in the sections that follow.

First, however, it is important to address the theme of managerial "buy-in," because it has a critical impact on all other themes. As we

Table 4.2 Ten Key Training Themes Identified in the Telephone Survey

Theme	Related question
Retention	How does employee turnover relate to an organization's commitment to training?
Cross-functional training	Are employees trained to perform multiple functions within the organization, and if so, why?
Employee motivation	Are employees motivated to participate in training?
Incentives	Does the organization reward employees for learning?
Transferability	Are the skills taught in training usable outside of the organization providing those skills?
Managerial buy-in	Do managers throughout the organization appreciate and stand behind the value of training?
Differences	Are there any major differences between the training provided to lower-wage employees and the training provided to all other employees?
Innovative training	Has the organization designed any novel approaches to training?
Technology	Does the organization use technology in the delivery of training?

SOURCE: Authors' analysis.

note in the definition of philosophy-driven organizations, there exists a culture of commitment to training within these organizations, because of both economic and sociopsychological factors. In these organizations, management promotes a culture of training and realizes its worth. Thus, managerial buy-in is rarely an obstacle to the provision of training to lower-wage employees. In market-driven organizations, on the other hand, only some managers have realized the positive effect of training on their organizations' bottom lines; they are likely to encourage training purely because of economic forces. Other managers in market-driven organizations have not realized the impact of training on the bottom-line and they may make it more difficult to provide training to all employees. Managers in nature-of-work-driven organizations also tend to focus on economic factors when considering training provision. Often when making training decisions, the nature-of-work-driven managers look first at the immediate impacts of disrupting an employees' production routine, rather than the longer-term impacts of providing training to that employee.

Table 4.3 Typical Perspectives on 10 Key Themes for Lower-Wage Worker Training

Criterion	Motivation category of organizations		
	Philosophy driven	Market driven	Nature-of-work driven
Managerial buy-in	Managers are key drivers behind the philosophy of the organization, so lack of buy-in is not an obstacle to overcome.	Some managers realize that to successfully deal with market fluctuations, they must support and encourage the training function.	Organizations struggle with managerial buy-in because managers rarely see the need to pull employees off the line or away from their daily tasks.
Retention	State explicitly that the philosophy of the organization recognizes training as an invaluable tool for recruitment and retention. Because of training, employees' perceptions of their workplace are improved and retention improves as a result.	Retention is often a problem; organizations are forced to train employees because of high turnover or because they realize they must train them in order to keep them.	Training is usually required by law or is so job-specific that it is difficult to view training as a retention tool.
Cross-functional training	Employees are trained to do other jobs within the organization, which helps them better understand the whole organization and how it operates.	Shortage of time and skills means that flexibility is not pursued via training as much as hiring/letting go or outsourcing.	Cross-functional training is often required by the nature of the work—especially in manufacturing firms. OJT cross-functional training is implemented in order to reduce slips in the production cycle.

(continued)

Table 4.3 (continued)

Criterion	Motivation category of organizations		
	Philosophy driven	Market driven	Nature-of-work driven
Employee motivation	Employees are highly motivated to participate in training because of the philosophy the organizations holds toward training.	Employees are not much motivated on their own to take part in training, but when managers buy into training, they help boost employees' motivations toward training.	In an environment often highly regulated or unionized, some employees seem to have longer-term engagements with the organization. Employees' desires to stay with the organization over time have a positive impact on their motivations to participate in training.
Incentives	Tangible and intangible incentives exist for employees to take part in training. Paths toward promotions or pay increases are clear.	The better organizations provide a clear explanation of the payoffs and rewards to training	Paths to promotion are often related to seniority, not performance, and any financial incentives to participate in training are small.
Transferability	Education and training give employees new skills to move beyond their current level of employment. Employees are encouraged to take advantage of programs offering skills to move them out of the lower-wage category.	Some language or literacy skills are provided, motivated by the employers' needs to maintain their workforces, not to improve the employees' marketability.	The nature of the work dictates that any time off the job for training strains the organization; providing skills beyond those required for the job is thus uncommon.
Formalization of on-the-job training	Most training is provided in a formal fashion; thus there is less focus on OJT training.	Because turnover is high and OJT training relatively inexpensive, OJT training is formalized.	The nature of the work is such that formal OJT training is very common.

Differences	There are no fundamental differences between training provided to lower-wage and higher-wage workers.	The content of courses usually varies by occupation level. Lower-wage employees receive more specific job-skill training as well as training required by outside regulatory entities.	Differences between higher- and lower-wage employees are generally vast.
Innovative training	Training is not limited to the bare minimum—innovative programs have been put into place and are well received by employees. Awards and recognition from outside organizations are not uncommon.	Training departments spend most of their time designing, developing, and delivering training in order to react to the market, not to preempt the market.	Innovative training programs are rare.
Technology	When appropriate, technology plays an important and useful role in the delivery of training.	Commonly these organizations are not yet ready to use technology to deliver training.	Training on technology is much more common than providing training through technology. However, when appropriate, CBT and other technologies are used to deliver training.

SOURCE: Authors' analysis.

GENERAL FINDINGS

We can summarize some general findings that emerged from the data gathered from and the discussions with the firms included in the telephone interviews:

- The mean reported percentage of an organization's workforce that is lower-wage is 44.3 percent, with a range of 10 to 93 percent.

- Most lower-wage employees are concentrated in positions that reflect the nature of the respondents' industry or business. For example, in lower-wage positions manufacturing organizations employ line workers, restaurants employ servers and cooks, and transportation companies employ bus drivers. Also, lower-wage positions tend to fall into entry-level, seasonal, and part-time categories.

- Over the past few years, most organizations have experienced little change in the proportion of their employees who occupy lower-wage positions as compared with higher-wage positions.

- Approximately 80 percent of the organizations use some type of technology to deliver training to their lower-wage workers.

- More than 95 percent of the surveyed organizations provide training for lower-wage workers on site.

- Typically, the responsibility for providing training to lower-wage employees is shared between the organization's human resources department and the departments in which the lower-wage employees work.

The discussion that follows draws on some of these findings while exploring the perspectives of employers in each of the three classification groups on questions central to the practice of providing training for lower-wage workers, including content, benefits, and barriers.

Training Content

We asked respondents what types of training they provide to their lower-wage employees. New-employee orientation represents one major component of most organizations' training initiatives. Interestingly, some organizations mentioned that they have started to promote employees from within their organizations in order to reduce their orientation training costs. Team building and customer service courses were also prevalent in many organizations, but especially within service industry organizations. Some training is required by law; among regulated courses, those on safety, diversity, and sexual harassment were the most often mentioned. External regulations appear to play a dual role—they represent a key impetus for firms to provide training, but a number of employers also noted that workers' motivation and interest in completing such courses is lower than it is for many other types of training.

For the most part, there were few surprises with regard to the types of training that organizations provide to their lower-wage staff. Curricula related to job skills and required and organization-wide courses were very common. However, a few innovative courses are worth noting:

- A number of organizations provide courses on general educational development (GED) and English as a second language (ESL) to people during work hours.

- One organization makes available 52 individual workshops to be taken during work hours. These workshops are aimed at developing people both professionally and personally, and cover such topics as organization skills, writing, listening skills, and conflict resolution. The curriculum feeds into the employees' professional development plans, which each employee and manager discuss twice a year. The outcomes of these meetings help to identify which workshops an employee should attend, and also allow the training and development department to determine which workshops to offer.

- One organization provides "transition training," knowing that employees at one point or another will leave the organization. The philosophy behind this training is that the organization wants to make sure that employees are prepared for this transition when it comes either through resignation or retirement. The training consists of courses on financial planning, health and wellness, leisure opportunities, and emotional preparation in order to avoid the "death after retirement" attitude.

We also asked employers to describe the percentage of training time that would fall into the following categories: personal skills courses, work-related courses, and other courses generally required for some or all employees. We found, however, that many organizations had difficulty breaking their training out by these categories, which they said overlapped a lot. On average, all three motivation groups categorized only 11 to 12 percent of their courses as providing personal skills. Within market-driven and nature-of-work-driven organizations, the average proportion of work-related skills was 64 and 74 percent, respectively, whereas philosophy-driven organizations claimed that only 36 percent of their courses provided work-related skills. Interesting, however, was the fact that the average percentage of required courses in philosophy-driven organizations was higher than the average of the other two types: 39 percent of courses were required in philosophy-driven organizations, and 24 and 21 percent, respectively, were required in market- and nature-of-work-driven organizations.

Personal skills training seemed a bit more distinct than the other two groups. For most organizations, this category contained courses on stress release, interpersonal relations (conflict resolution), English as a second language, and computer skills (when not directly job related). Most also commented that personal skills courses were often the ones offered on a voluntary basis.

Questions about the voluntary or mandatory status of a course revealed that many organizations offered no voluntary training opportunities to lower-wage workers. Those that did offer such opportunities tended to focus on basic skills acquisition (such as GED or ESL programs) and on courses that generally helped qualify an employee for a promotion or a new position.

Within those that did offer voluntary training, tangible incentives to participate most often included pay raises and promotions. Only 5 percent of the 40 organizations provided cash bonuses to employees who voluntarily trained to become certified with new skills. Most courses offered by all organizations, however, were mandatory in nature.

Overall, the content of training did not differ greatly among the three motivation groups. Cross-functional training, however (training on functions other than the employee's own) and the formalization of on-the-job training as related to training content differed according to the motivations behind the provision of training. In the case of philosophy-driven organizations, lower-wage employees were more likely to receive cross-functional training because employers recognized the intellectual value of such training to employees. When employees were knowledgeable about job functions other than their own, they felt more valued by their employers. In these firms, the culture of promoting training throughout the organization helped produce better-motivated employees. Nature-of-work-driven organizations, on the other hand, provided cross-training to lower-wage employees because, without it, their production cycles were more likely to suffer economically. For example, manufacturing firms may cross-train front-line employees so that those employees may cover for one another should one not be able to work during any given shift. Finally, cross-functional training was quite absent in market-driven firms. Such firms typically found it much easier to provide consistent training content to specific groups of employees, and would look to outside sources (whether through outsourcing or new hires) to fill skill gaps.

The economic-driven types of organizations rely more heavily on formalized on-the-job training (OJT) than do philosophy-driven organizations. Market-driven organizations realize that the costs of formal OJT are low, and nature-of-work-driven organizations find it efficient to formalize OJT. Philosophy-driven organizations, however, generally provide formalized training; they present formal content through organized courses, whether through classrooms or on the job. Although they do provide training through the job, their reliance upon this method is not as heavy as it is for their market-driven counterparts.

Differences in Training for Lower-Wage Workers

Respondents were asked if the training content provided to lower-wage employees differed in any way from the training provided to other employees. For the most part, they reported that content was perhaps the most important difference between the training for the two different groups of workers. Most frequently, the reported reason behind this variance was that different groups of employees need different skills. However, the reasoning behind such a statement varied across the three different types of organizations we interviewed. Philosophy-driven organizations were more likely to respond that there were no differences in training opportunities provided to various employee groups, and tended to cite deeply held organizational commitments to providing training to the organizations' entire workforces as the reason behind this answer. For example, one philosophy-driven employer stated that "we have a philosophy that training will be provided across the board: if the CEO gets a certain type of training, everyone gets it." This respondent did acknowledge that there might be varying levels of skill that are taught during these courses, but the underlying principle—that all employees are entitled to equal training opportunities—was the most important factor for this organization. Strong support from top managers was an integral component of this philosophy. Not only did it help promote a sense of equity across employees, but it likely helped to ensure that the necessary resources were available to provide such across-the-board training.

By contrast, market- and nature-of-work-driven organizations were more likely to report important differences in the training provided to different groups of employees. The manufacturing, technology, services, and health care industries that make up large portions of these groups account for some of this difference, particularly within the nature-of-work-driven organizations. Because lower-wage employees were typically found in entry-level and front-line positions, more safety and other regulated training was required of them, whereas employees at higher-wage levels were not as likely to take part in such courses. Representatives of market-driven organizations commonly explained that, although course content did not vary across employee groups, courses were sometimes customized to skill levels and language abilities. Most often, customized training courses were provided to lower-wage workers because they were more likely to require extra focus on basic skills, such as reading, and to require that courses be translated into other languages. At the other end of the spectrum, there were organizations that acknowledged that training opportunities are "much better for the 'haves' than for the 'have-nots.'"

While most respondents focused on the *content* of training when responding to the question of whether there were differences among employee groups, there were a few respondents whose answers fell into a different category. For example, one reported finding value in using different media (such as technology-delivered training) to deliver training to lower-wage employees because such media were more adaptable to the needs of some of these employees for slower-paced instruction. Another respondent, taking exactly the opposite perspective, stated that technology-delivered training did not work for their lower-wage employees and is made available only for training other categories of employees.

Philosophy- and nature-of-work-driven organizations tended to use technology to deliver training more often than their market-driven counterparts. One explanation for this difference may be the ease with which these types of organizations acquired resources to invest in technology to deliver training. Whether resources were more easily acquired because of consistent and reliable managerial buy-in, or because job functions necessitated training through technology, providers of training in these types of organizations were more able to promote the value in technology-delivered training.

Another question asked during the survey revealed that practically all the respondents would like to provide more training to lower-wage workers. This was perhaps not surprising, given that our survey respondents were primarily trainers. Most said that, in an ideal world, the training they would add would include more of the types of training already offered—additional personal and basic skills training and refresher courses. A few respondents did believe that their organizations currently provide more than adequate levels of training; they were more concerned with getting people to take advantage of the training opportunities already available.

Training Practices

The firms included in the telephone survey reported that the amount of training they provided to lower-wage workers was increasing. Many organizations in the telephone survey reported that their needs were changing, with new requirements for a more educated workforce. They also reported that they were seeking ways to overcome problems created by a job market in which it had become more difficult to find skilled workers. It was not universally true, however, that the pressure for more training was growing. For example, one respondent remarked, "I'd rather have one employee off the floor [for lack of training] than two [because the trainer must leave his station to train that person]."

The act of tracking the training provided was becoming more common and more consistent within the training departments surveyed. Using such measures as class hours, attendance, and expenditures, 62 percent of respondents tracked the amount of training they provided to lower-wage employees. Increases in employee turnover, as well as external factors (such as increased auditing), have contributed to an increased focus on tracking training. One respondent reported, "Tracking helps predict future needs and is used in performance evaluations; it adds to the hiring process, helps determine the types of training that are necessary, is used in justifying training and development's existence, and is used in showing that training proactively enhances employees' job performance."

We found that the three types of organizations tracked training for different reasons. Philosophy-driven organizations formally tracked training to help plan for future training needs and to link employee participation and course completion to incentives or promotions. Market-driven organizations were more likely than their philosophy-driven counterparts to use informal means to track training, or not to track it at all. However, market-driven organizations also claimed that their tracking had increased over recent years, perhaps because of more pressure from management to "justify" the value of training. Finally, nature-of-work-driven organizations more commonly tracked training in order to report to outside regulatory or monitoring agencies that their employees had completed certain courses. For example, one company explained that they tracked who had been trained in order to maintain their ISO 9000 compliance, while another explained that employees must complete certain courses and achieve specific scores in order to remain qualified for their positions.

Benefits of Training Lower-Wage Workers

From the organizational perspective, the most frequently mentioned benefits of training lower-wage employees included improvement in work quality, customer service, and employee recruitment and retention. Other common organizational benefits were better safety and error records, increased employee satisfaction, and improved employee morale. Again, although there was little difference in the answers given by representatives of the three different types of organizations in this category of questions, the motivations behind their answers were different. The philosophy-driven organizations were more likely to realize that they could use training proactively to improve employee retention and motivation. Two of the most enthusiastic responses to our questions on the benefits of training came, for example, from the philosophy-driven group:

- "We get improved productivity, better service, increased revenues, increased sales, decreased accidents, and better retention. Training drives the business and improves the company's image within the community."

- "We benefit from a higher degree of valuable competencies, self-esteem and morale increase, employees feel valued, absenteeism declines, safety and morale improve together, and we get better productivity and quality through providing training."

Market-driven and nature-of-work-driven organizations, by contrast, took a more reactionary view toward training. One market-driven organization saw the benefits only as very limited: "Training is one way to make sure that we keep the certification we get every year from a governmental agency."

Barriers and Enablers

Often firms realized the organizational benefits cited above only after facing and overcoming a wide variety of obstacles. Importantly, when we asked the respondents what enablers or barriers they faced in providing training, most focused on a discussion of barriers. All three categories of organizations faced similar barriers.

The lack of time available to employees for training was a barrier cited by many employers (we discuss it in more detail in our descriptions of the case studies in the third phase of this study). Usually the time barriers were the result of production, service, or delivery schedules, fully employed staffs, and the training schedule.

Cost concerns were also frequently mentioned. Another common barrier was language, with literacy issues often mentioned alongside the language barrier. A number of respondents noted that some of their lower-wage employees lacked the skills and abilities expected upon hiring. They also noted difficulty sometimes in overcoming employees' negative attitudes, to get them to benefit from the training they received.

One market-driven organization and five nature-of-work-driven organizations mentioned the problem of getting managers to buy into training. For many, this issue is closely related to the issues of time and cost: our interviews often turned to the importance of managerial buy-in during discussions of time or cost issues. One manufacturing organization explained, "we meet with success about 85 percent of the time when the tactic is to convince managers to take a chance and allow training. But, we [as trainers] have to bow to production, because no matter what, it always comes first." Certainly, the nature of some organizations creates an environment where it is more difficult to pull an employee from his or her job for a training course. When firms are short of staff, it is even more difficult to gain support for training. Sometimes, creative scheduling and flexible training staffs are easier fixes than gaining managerial buy-in. But numerous organizations uphold the belief that managerial buy-in is the key to the success of an organization's training program. These organizations generally maintain communication with managers, build partnerships throughout their organizations (especially with people at the top), and work to explain the short- and long-term benefits of training.

Other methods mentioned as ways of overcoming barriers to training were to increase the frequency of training, to remain flexible in scheduling the times for courses, to vary the lengths of courses, to provide translations, and to teach language and basic skills courses.

Employers' Assessments of What Works

Forty-seven percent of the firms responded that they formally assessed the impact of their training programs. Their methods ranged from completely informal to formal Kirkpatrick (1998) models. The respondents were also asked for their opinions on what general characteristics of training for lower-wage workers tended to produce the best results. Keeping in mind that these answers are opinions, it is interesting to note that relatively "good" training was often related to courses presented in a manner "closer to real life," as well as to those with energetic instructors, those in which participation was encouraged, and those in which class length was short. But when asked about the characteristics of courses that proved challenging, some respondents found that classroom and lecture-delivered courses were not always well received, that soft skills were difficult to teach, and that employees did poorly at retaining content presented in a passive manner.

Employees' Feedback on Lower-Wage Training

Employers were also asked what feedback they receive from employees who participate in training. The most common response was that employees were excited about the promotional opportunities and personal growth that go along with the various training programs available to them. This was true within all three categories of organizations. Linking training to promotion and pay increases was a common practice throughout the organizations surveyed. Other positive, but less common, feedback included simple enjoyment of the courses, general interest in doing a good job, and improved teamwork abilities.

Of the philosophy-driven organizations that responded to this question, none reported negative feedback. However, the picture was a bit different for some of the other respondents. Some, in both the market- and nature-of-work-driven organizations, reported receiving less than enthusiastic feedback regarding the training they provide to lower-wage employees. For example, one employer said that training was always the first thing to get dropped when an employee had other things come up. Others mentioned that employees sometimes felt a lack of managerial support that would encourage them to take advantage of a company education program. One respondent mentioned that employees who did not participate (a majority in that case) generally lacked any desire to advance or improve their own skills (although that particular employer offered no incentives for employees to participate in the voluntary training). Such comments are particularly notable given that we expected to receive predominantly positive responses from trainers describing the reaction of employees to their training opportunities.

Macroeconomic and Other External Motivating Factors

We asked respondents about the role of external forces, such as the economic environment, in shaping their training strategies for their lower-wage workers. Among the range of responses were the following:

- "The tight labor market has forced us to focus more on modifying or customizing training for lower levels of education and on providing new basic skills training."

- "Turnover and the tight labor market have made it necessary to train people more quickly and thoroughly in order to get them onto the job as soon as possible. We cannot afford to have people in training too long, but if the labor market loosens, we'd expect training to become a little longer again, and more focused on developing skills once an employee is in the field."

- "Our practices haven't changed, but they should. We're getting a less-skilled class of employees in new hires today than five years ago, and the employees that we're retaining often do not have the basic skills they need or that this group used to have."

- "There has been a dispute between human resources staffing and training. HR is sending us the 'leftovers' and training has needed to tighten up and become more of a weeding-out entity. This probably isn't too bad a situation, because it's in training that we can really tell who is going to work out and who is not. In essence, training has become the 'screen' for finding worthy employees, rather than their initial entrance test."

We then asked respondents the following question: "If the labor market were to loosen, would the changes made in reaction to its tightening remain in place?" Representative answers reveal a fascinating variety of perspectives:

- "Yes. Training is becoming an identity and more people want the skills [we provide]."

- "Yes. We will continue to strive to maintain and improve our workforce's excellence and competencies."

- "No. If the labor market loosens, we could spend more time developing skills in the field. We wouldn't necessarily change training courses, but the time spent in on-the-job training would increase."

- "No. We would expect things to slow down a little so that we could have more time to implement training."

The frantic pace created by a tight labor market certainly created a sort of Catch-22 situation. On the one hand, organizations were forced to rise to the challenge of providing quick turnaround training so that production schedules could be maintained. On the other hand, the tight labor market meant that longer-term training was needed to remedy skills deficits among the workers available to the organization.

In addition to macroeconomic factors, respondents mentioned a number of other external forces affecting training practices, such as cultural diversity, education gaps, the use of technology, increased competition, the ability to use multimedia to deliver courses, and increased regulatory constraints.

CONCLUSIONS AND DISCUSSION

It is important to remember first of all that the telephone survey responses on which we base these conclusions involved 40 organizations that we had initially chosen as providing an above-average level of lower-wage training. The survey revealed that, even within this group, there is a wide range of practices and policies with regard to training for lower-wage employees. Some organizations provided the bare minimum of training to their employees—in those, the training required by law was the only training lower-wage employees ever received. At the other end of the spectrum are a few organizations with a deeply held belief that training is good. In those organizations, all employees, regardless of their position, received the exact same training, and were actively encouraged to seek growth-oriented training opportunities on their own.

The tight labor market that prevailed at the time of the interviews definitely affected training practices for lower-wage workers. Again, this took different forms in different organizations. Some organizations viewed this market as an opportunity to use training to ensure that their current employees did not leave, while others cut back their training to make sure that their production lines did not shut down because of high turnover rates. Some organizations reported that electronic learning technologies provided highly effective methods for delivering training; others reported that they were unsuccessful in using such methods.

One important insight emerges from the telephone surveys: There is no evidence that employer concern about losing workers after (and perhaps because of) providing general education and training was a major impediment to its provision. In fact, most respondents interviewed in the telephone surveys indicated just the opposite—that by providing education and training to lower-wage workers, they were able to improve worker retention rates. It may be that training is functioning as a form of fringe benefit for employees, rather than representing purely a method for the organization to improve the skills of its workforce.

Nevertheless, it is likely that the costs that employers incur in providing education and training remain a barrier to its provision. While virtually none of the employers interviewed in the telephone surveys mentioned the *direct cost* of providing training, concern about the *opportunity cost* (lost productivity while workers are away from the job) was mentioned by some. This suggests that it is important that any public policy interventions be mindful of employers' concerns that learning be delivered flexibly, with minimal lost productivity (for example, giving workers access to learning, particularly if "developmental" in nature, either before or after work hours).

One of the most promising possibilities for reducing the "costs" of education and training (from both the employers' and the employees' perspectives) is the use of electronic learning technologies. Although the fixed costs of developing high-quality content for electronic delivery can be quite high, the marginal costs of delivering it are very low. Evidence both from the telephone surveys and from the case studies in phase 3, however, indicate only mixed success in attempts to use electronic learning technologies to deliver learning to the lower-wage workforce. This is discussed further in the phase 3 chapters.

In summation, of the 40 firms we surveyed in the phase 2 telephone interviews, eight appeared to be making extraordinarily high levels of investment in lower-wage worker training. We selected those eight firms for the site visits and case studies that formed phase 3 of our study. Chapters 5 through 10 discuss those findings.

Note

1. Certainly these motivating factors often overlap. Nevertheless, we tried to assign each firm to one group in order to clarify the roles of each factor most effectively.

Phase 3: Case Studies

5
Boeing Employees' Credit Union

The Boeing Employees' Credit Union (BECU) is located in Tuk-wila, Washington. BECU, a not-for-profit financial cooperative (owned by members of the credit union), started serving the financial needs of Boeing employees and their families in 1936. By the time of our study BECU had grown to become the third-largest credit union in the United States and the largest in Washington State, holding assets over $2.8 billion and with over 290,000 members.[1] Its size makes it a direct competitor of large national banks and brokerage institutions. Because of its not-for-profit, membership-based status, BECU does not compete with other credit unions. Indeed, much like the LYNX public transportation organization (see Chapter 8), BECU is frequently able to share information, best practices, and training ideas with other comparable organizations.

BECU's mission is to "join persons of a common bond into an organization that will provide a balanced program of quality savings, loans, and other financial services to the membership" (BECU 2000). Existing alongside this mission, according to the vice president of human resources, is the traditional credit union philosophy of "people helping people." As a result, "what has made BECU stand out is the service we offer to the member."[2] This general emphasis on service thus exists on both a day-to-day basis and a larger scale. This principle also helps to support the organization's efforts to improve the financial understanding of its members. For example, in recent years BECU created a network of educational express service centers to educate members about remote services and the available products and services BECU offers. This focus, in turn, supports the credit union's philosophy and business objectives, while a focus on providing opportunities for its employees is a logical complement to this orientation.

THE WORKFORCE

At the time of our study about 60 percent of BECU's approximately 850 employees were "staff employees," meaning that they worked in front-line positions as, for example, call center customer service representatives, member service representatives, tellers, or processing representatives. Approximately 50 percent of the front-line staff were earning wages at or below $10 per hour. In terms of job tenure, nearly 60 percent of BECU's employees had been at the organization for three years or less, and 10 percent had over 10 years of service. A high school diploma was required of almost all employees, with the exception of some part-time interns.

Unlike many of the organizations we visited during this study, BECU reported no significant adverse effect from the prevailing tight labor market (the unemployment rate in Seattle in July 2000 was 3.6 percent) in terms of the organization's ability to attract and retain good employees. BECU's capacity to avoid the effects of what may be the most common labor market problem reported in the current economic environment may be traced to a number of advantages held by the organization: a strong reputation in the community, powerful and positive recognition of the Boeing name, and positive word-of-mouth impressions from current employees regarding their experiences at BECU. In fact, some employees with whom we spoke commented that they'd been trying to "get a foot in the door" at BECU for some time; even before applying for a job, they had heard many positive things about the organization and what a good place it was to work at. To this reputation can be added the advantages of a deliberately family-friendly work environment and an emphasis on opportunities for career advancement, as well as for learning and education.

Nevertheless, recruitment and retention remained a focus at BECU. The director of training observed that, regardless of labor market conditions, a primary challenge was always to keep good employees and maintain low turnover. Indeed, given the importance of quality customer service to BECU's business success, it was clear that recruitment and retention, as well as employee development, were high priorities for the organization.

EDUCATION AND TRAINING INITIATIVES

Over time, the responsibilities for job-specific training at BECU shifted from being decentralized (at the individual departmental level), to centralized (at the corporate level), and then decentralized again. At the time of our study, the corporate training department had responsibility for all *company-wide required training*, voluntary courses, tuition reimbursement, and general financial industry courses (such as sales training and credit union financials). Each department was responsible for providing all *job-specific training* for individuals working within each department. In other words, departments were responsible for training people how to do their jobs, while the corporate training department provided courses that complemented and enhanced an employee's work. The corporate training department also provided training on issues that cut across the organization. For example, corporate training provided training on technology and new product or service roll-outs, which certainly affected employees' job performance. In recent years, BECU had also shifted its focus away from take-home, self-study courses back to more interactive and traditional methods of training. One exception to this shift was the increased availability of computer- and Web-based, self-study training. This exception points to the training department's commitment to responding flexibly to the needs of the organization and recognizing what types of training work well. The focus of our visit to BECU was on the training that the corporate training department provided. The mission of this BECU unit is stated as follows: "Because we believe in the ultimate potential of every employee, we provide opportunities for self-discovery, along with personal and professional growth, that contribute to the overall success of BECU" (BECU 2000).

The training curriculum, a combination of mandatory and voluntary courses, was offered during business hours in the corporate offices and sometimes in staff locations.[3] Classes were delivered using traditional classroom techniques as well as computer-based training, and the training department used an intranet to assist in training delivery as well. The company had no clear evidence of which method was generally most effective. In the future, as the company becomes more dependent upon e-commerce and open finance, it would like to be able to make additional use of various forms of technology-based training. New-employee orientation was mandatory for all employees. All front-line workers were strongly encouraged to participate in BECU's service excellence program. BECU worked much as the Wyoming Student Loan Corporation (see Chapter 10) did in that the customer service requirements of its call center provided an initial information base in the process of educating most new employees on the overall workings of the organization. The call center had a separate and extensive orientation and training program that lasted a total of five weeks, which, in addition to the organization's new-employee orientation program (conducted by the corporate training department) included job-specific training, time in the coaching lab, and mentoring time for the new employee. The call center created the curriculum for specific job skills training, while corporate training provided the customer service component of the training to call center employees. The corporate training department curriculum provided an overall introduction to the business of the credit union and the skills necessary to handle member inquiries: the credit union's mission and purpose, the foundation and history of its operations, BECU's service expectations, employee procedures, and various other aspects of the business. These training components were structured to be taken alongside the new employee's departmental (job-specific) training.

Many employees began their careers at BECU in the call center, often before moving on to jobs in other departments. The knowledge base that call center employees gained in their departmental orientation made them prime candidates to fill open positions at BECU. In fact, the call center became such a major source for other departments looking to fill job openings that in 1998 BECU adopted a requirement that employees must spend at least one year in the call center before moving to another department. Well-defined career paths complemented this framework, which helped the organization keep employees by providing a formal structure for advancement for employees who moved into new departments after "learning the ropes" in the call center. Thus, by providing employees with incentives to stay at the company, BECU also improved its capacity to derive greater benefits from the training that it provided.

The director of training estimated that 80 to 90 percent of staff employees take advantage of voluntary courses in order to acquire new skills and move up within the organization. Courses entitled "Service Excellence," "Solutions to Service Challenges," and "Working Through It Together—Diversity" were officially voluntary courses, but were strongly recommended by managers. A key to the high participation rates was the communication of information related to training. Monthly calendars of course offerings were made available to all employees, and in general, department managers were seen as good about keeping their employees informed about opportunities provided by the training department. In fact, some departments had created job descriptions to include suggestions that employees take certain courses in order to be eligible for promotions.

Another incentive BECU offered for its training opportunities was tuition reimbursement. The program was generous, with no annual limit to the amount of reimbursement an employee may receive, and all employees had access to the program. The content of the courses taken had to be approved by managers, but they were flexible when determining which courses provided the skills that would benefit the credit union. Interestingly, however, overall expenses for the tuition reimbursement program were lower than the national average, according to the data provided ASTD. During our study, about 14 percent of the staff (120 employees) were participating in the tuition reimbursement program. According to BECU, this percentage had been higher in the past.

Overall, BECU made a substantial financial commitment to its various training offerings, with expenditures (measured per employee) more than double the industry average and significantly higher than the national average as well (again, according to ASTD data). The percentage of employees who received training, close to 100 percent, was also higher than comparable averages, as was the trainer-to-employee ratio.

Management Perspectives

When asked about the importance BECU placed on its training programs, both the vice president of human resources and the director of training expressed similar views. Discussing the organizational benefits of training in terms of employee satisfaction, development, and retention, both felt that, especially for lower-wage employees, the opportunities for advancement through education were seen as a significant benefit of working for an organization like BECU. The credit union's focus on providing education to its members complemented the provision of educational opportunities for all employees, as did the belief that increasing employee knowledge would truly lead to better service to members. According to the vice president of human resources, all training provided by BECU was directly tied into the organization's objectives. As this book was being written, the BECU training and development department was creating competencies for each job description to further strengthen that relationship by allowing the acquisition of new skills to be tied back into performance management and the appraisal system.

Every training session was evaluated at Kirkpatrick's levels 1 and 2. The processes for evaluating courses at levels 3 and 4 were created in 1999, and they have since been tested in a few situations, but at the time of writing, there was no formal, consistent process in place for level 3 and 4 evaluation. One of the main goals for 2001 was to implement those two levels of evaluations on a more consistent basis, but gaining adequate cooperation and support from individual departments had been a struggle. Until recently, management had relied on informal feedback and thanks from employees and supervisors to monitor the usefulness and effectiveness of training on the job. In the opinion of the director of training, customer service and software courses had been particularly successful and well liked by students. Not surprisingly, departmental managers, on the other hand, expressed particular appreciation for the courses focused on providing and strengthening those skills that are most relevant to an employee's everyday work, such as the "Writing a Better Letter" course and the Microsoft software courses.

Like many training departments, BECU's training and development department faced the challenge of trying to get various departments within the organization to fully embrace the training function. BECU's corporate training department made a significant effort to communicate to managers and supervisors the value of training, especially for some of the courses offered to employees on a voluntary basis. (The development of an evaluation process through which results might be shared with supervisors was expected to help in this effort.) While sending this message to supervisors, the corporate training staff also hoped to eradicate some employees' perceptions that their supervisors would not allow them to take part in voluntary training. Consistent with this goal, the vice president of human resources met with all new employees within their first six months on the job to welcome them to the organization as well as to discuss the opportunities available to them through the training department.

Employee Perspectives

We spoke with eight employees representing various departments, levels of pay, and lengths of service. Almost all the employees with whom we spoke anticipated staying at BECU for a long time, saying that it was a good ("great") place to work. Even one who did not anticipate a long-term career with BECU agreed that "the Credit Union is great," but then noted, "but I don't intend to stay here forever." Five of the eight had changed positions within the organization during their service, with the call center being the starting point for three of the five. (Notably, the three who started in the call center were all aware that it was the place to "get your foot in the door.")

In general, all the employees interviewed spoke highly of the training they had received. One employee, who had started at BECU before the job-specific training had been devolved back to individual departments, claimed that it had been hard to learn the ropes when she first started and that training had not been well organized. However, with the change in the structure of training, "training is much better now." This employee also noted that "some of my colleagues believe that the benefits at BECU are not great, but the training opportunities make up for that." Other employees noted that their supervisors were quite supportive of the various training opportunities available to the employees, and remarked on the existence of "a lot of internal effort to treat employees the same way that members are treated." Employees also noted their appreciation of courses focused on "portable" job skills, such as writing business letters and providing customer service.

Although the overall attitude held toward training opportunities was positive, some employees did voice concern. A few mentioned that scheduling class participation was sometimes difficult, especially for those who worked in branches relatively far away from the corporate offices where training was provided. Some also noted that the nature of some jobs, such as call center representatives or tellers, made it more difficult to schedule training than it was for positions with less customer interaction.

With regard to the generous tuition reimbursement policy, the employees typically expressed a range of feelings and knowledge. For example, one employee explained that her supervisor advised her to "go get your degree, have us pay for it, then leave." On the other hand, one employee was neither familiar with the policy nor interested in it.

Three employees mentioned one particular course that was of interest: the "career pathing" course, which helped employees define the occupations they might want to move into at BECU. During the course, participants assessed their skills and weaknesses, evaluated their own performances, and identified their values. The course also involved being matched with a mentor inside BECU, giving insights and further understanding of that mentor's career.

Overall, these employees were happy with the environment in which they worked. A couple of them noted that the organization had become more employee-focused during the time they had worked at BECU, and that the organization had become more willing to work around employees' personal needs: "They don't force you to choose between your job and your family." The culture was described as "very friendly" and as one where "people were willing to go the extra mile for both employees and members."

LESSONS LEARNED

After a number of structural changes, BECU had developed an extremely rational process for the delivery of much of its mandatory training. BECU achieved efficiency by presenting this core information (such as information about the organization, its procedures, and its customers, as well as industry-related information) through the single orientation program offered by corporate training, which all new employees attend. This provided a useful base of common knowledge for new employees, while simultaneously presenting them with a logical structure for the start of careers that might move into other departments. Despite the expected bumps due to the difficulty of having one department serve as the organization's *de facto* feeding ground for other departments, many employees nonetheless reported that their supervisors were generally supportive of training opportunities and the promotions to which they might ultimately lead. The "career pathing" course supported this overall structure and provided employees with formal tools that could be used in evaluating their potential careers inside BECU. Although not all organizations could support such a structure, there are significant benefits evident for those that can.

BECU can boast other successes as well. Since it tends not to compete with other credit unions, the organization has been able to share its courses with other credit unions. In fact, the Washington Credit Union League (WCUL), of which BECU is a member, asked BECU to teach its Service Excellence course at the WCUL conference to other members, many of which are much smaller. BECU has also received requests from individual credit unions for help developing certain types of training. The interest of external organizations in the courses and methods developed by BECU reflects the benefits of BECU's relatively large size (which helps to provide the resources necessary to develop courses internally) and, more importantly, its capacity and willingness to take advantage of that size to make a commitment to developing a broad range of training courses, both mandatory and voluntary.

Overall, BECU validates many of the lessons that are seen in other organizations. A management representative noted that BECU is accountable for ensuring a return to its membership, with training representing one of the ways that the organization can improve its service and return to its members. Like UPMC-Passavant (see Chapter 9), BECU puts an emphasis on treating employees the same as it treats customers (members), providing an additional foundation for the organization's employee-friendly training opportunities, especially given the organization's commitment to member education. Similarly, as a service-oriented organization, BECU represents another example of the central role that training can play in enhancing the skills of its employees to ensure that customers receive high-quality service from the front-line workers that make up most of the organization's employees.

Notes

1. Although BECU has members from throughout the United States and the world, most reside in the greater Puget Sound area.
2. This and other such quotes, both direct and indirect, are taken from our notes made during the various case study interviews.
3. Most of the training was offered in two separate corporate facilities. One training facility housed the training department and the customer call center, which was not accessible to BECU members. The other training facility was the main member center, which also housed the management functions. Employees from the satellite member service centers located throughout the metropolitan Seattle region usually had to go to the corporate facilities for training that was outside of their department's responsibilities.

6
CVS Corporation

CVS Corporation opened as Consumer Value Store in Lowell, Massachusetts, in 1963. Since then, the chain, headquartered in Woonsocket, Rhode Island, has become the nation's largest retail drug merchant (measured by number of stores and prescriptions dispensed) by adding services (pharmacies were introduced to the stores in 1968) and acquiring drugstore chains (such as Peoples, Revco, and Arbor Drugs). At the time of our visit, there were over 4,000 CVS drugstores in 29 states and Washington, D.C., reflecting CVS's operating philosophy that when the company enters a new market, it enters it "with a bang," opening from 10 to 15 new stores at one time. The chain employed nearly 100,000 people, and in 1999 sales were over $18 billion.[1]

Our visit to a CVS store in downtown Boston, Massachusetts, differed in a few important ways from the other site visits that we conducted throughout this study. First, because CVS is a leader in working with government programs to provide career paths and training to some lower-wage employees, we focused much of our attention on that aspect of CVS's training strategy. In addition to speaking with a management representative, we spoke with an on-site trainer, a store manager, and various lower-wage employees. Thus, our discussion focuses on both traditional training issues and key observations related to the various programs in which CVS has partnered with state and local government organizations. Second, because of the retail nature of the organization, we visited a field site, not the corporate offices, in order to be able to speak with lower-wage workers. This provided a different perspective on the organization from the one we would have had from visiting the headquarters.

CVS believes its training needs are unique within the chain-drug industry. Driven in part by the market saturation strategies it employs and the exclusive nature of its contracts with many insurers, CVS has a per-store pharmaceutical volume that is much higher than at many other large drugstore chains. High volume for the pharmacy translates into higher volume for other parts of the store, as well. These factors help to drive the nature of the training that CVS provides to all employees who have customer contact. Two qualities made CVS a particularly interesting case study. First, it provided entry-level workers with training that appeared to be more systematic and formal than the training that such workers receive in most retail establishments. Second, the organization's focus on qualifying for tax credits and grants under various government programs enhanced the benefits of the structured training programs that it designed to retain and expand the potential of entry-level employees. Recent improvements to entry-level training programs appeared to have had benefits beyond those expected by CVS when the changes were initially made.

CVS GOVERNMENT PROGRAMS DEPARTMENT

It is important to understand the nature both of the CVS Government Programs Department and of the public sector initiatives to which CVS was responding in creating that department. Various "Welfare-to-Work" provisions of the Personal Responsibility and Work Opportunity Act (PRWORA) of 1996 gave rise to a host of programs at the federal, state, and local levels that were designed to encourage companies to hire former welfare recipients and provide them with career opportunities. Much of the funding for those programs (at all levels of government) can be traced to federal incentive block grants to the states. The incentives provided to enterprises typically take the form of tax credits or grants to create certain training programs or tracks. Similar programs exist on a smaller scale for other populations that are seen as disadvantaged in some way.

CVS began exploring such programs as potential vehicles for finding an untapped source of new employees in an increasingly tight labor market. A management representative responsible for CVS's participation in some of these programs observed that the programs were particularly helpful to CVS, given the tight labor market that then prevailed. Because of the success that CVS has had with such programs, she reported that it was unlikely that such collaborations would be dropped in the future even if the labor market were to expand, since the rate of retention for employees hired through Welfare-to-Work or similar programs was significantly greater than the retention rate for the overall employee population.

When CVS first started exploring these government avenues for finding and recruiting employees, the few department employees working on the project were able to identify, relatively easily, about $6 to $7 million in potential tax credits for CVS through various block grant incentive programs. Once the company realized that such funding was only the proverbial tip of the iceberg, it devoted more resources to the department. At the time of our study, there were seven government programs managers, each with responsibility for a specific region, who tracked and responded to national, state, and local laws that create opportunities for partnerships or grants within those regions.

Simultaneously, CVS recognized the need to develop, for store positions, training that was more responsive to the needs of a growing organization. This reflected the organization's realization that, as the number of stores increased, along with the volume of business they produced, the availability of qualified applicants would decrease. Creating clearly defined career paths with multiple levels of responsibility not only qualified CVS for government-sponsored grants and partnerships, but it also addressed the needs of the staff of two key areas within store operations—the pharmacy technicians and the photo lab operators. These were the two primary paths that the organization promoted at that time to its government funders and partners. Although motivated by the desire to qualify for public funding, CVS designed these paths to be accessible to any employee, not just to those associated with government programs. Because only (at most) a few pharmacy technicians and photo lab operators were needed per store, only about 25 percent of store employees took part in such programs.

THE WORKFORCE

Generally, the lower-wage staff of CVS was made up almost entirely of employees who did not hold supervisory positions. Those individuals included cashiers, stockers, photo lab operators, and pharmacy technicians, and they typically started at a minimum wage for entry-level workers. At the Boston site we visited, many employees were students, and many others had come to CVS from other retail organizations. The store manager at this site told us that he hires a core staff of full-time employees, or shift leaders, but that most of his workforce was made up of part-timers from whom he generally expected frequent turnover. He always had a "help wanted" sign in the front window of the store, and kept his eyes open for good workers in the area's other retail and fast-food chains whom he might be able to recruit. Noting that people at this wage level (starting at around minimum wage, or $6 per hour) and in these positions will change jobs for the difference of 25 cents per hour, the store manager pointed out that keeping his store fully staffed was an ongoing struggle, so routine that he saw it as a fundamental part of his job.

The consistently high turnover among lower-wage, entry-level employees made it quite difficult, from a business perspective, to justify the dedication of significant resources to training. Although considerable effort and resources were devoted to training professional and managerial staff, new employees hired off the street for front-line, "floor" jobs received only an orientation to CVS and training on the operation of the cash registers.

Some opportunities for advancement existed for front-line employees. For example, cashiers or stockers could move into managing certain sections of the store (such as the greeting cards or cosmetics sections), where their responsibilities included ordering inventory and maintaining the displays of those sections. Another common promotion for hourly employees was a move from part-time to full-time positions. To receive health care benefits, employees had to be classified as full-time and work at least 30 hours per week. (Other benefits, such as a retirement savings plan, were available to part-time employees who had at least 1,000 hours of service annually.) Each store manager determined how many full- and part-time staff that store would employ, so this decision depended heavily on each store's needs and its abilities to support a given staff composition.

CVS attracted employees through the School-to-Career, Welfare-to-Work, and Seniors-to-Work initiatives, with most coming through the Welfare-to-Work program. Such programs attract workers with a wide range of skills and abilities, so CVS worked with its partnering organizations (which include government agencies directly or other organizations, such as Goodwill Industries) to provide everything from job readiness skills to customer service and store operations skills to these employees. CVS has found particular success in working to bring people from these programs into its pharmacy technician and photo lab operator tracks, partly because the training available for such positions is well defined and thorough relative to other in-store positions.

EDUCATION AND TRAINING INITIATIVES

The standard training provided to lower-wage employees at CVS was delivered in one of two ways: through either individual trainers or regional learning centers (RLCs).

In the past, training at CVS was relatively centralized, with all training design and development done at headquarters, and most of the training aimed at managerial and professional staff. People in front-line positions received an orientation through CVS's Vista training program and also some on-the-job training. The latter was likely to be conducted by the store manager or more seasoned coworkers, typically at some point during the new hires' first few days of work. Unfortunately, new hire training was not always delivered in a systematic or timely manner, and the on-the-job training did not allow for a very comfortable transition for a new employee into the CVS workplace.

Ultimately, the organization determined that this training was not cost-effective in markets where employee turnover was high. At the time of our study, training curricula were developed at the corporate headquarters and rolled out to the field through RLCs or individual trainers who traveled to multiple store locations in a given geographic area, providing training to new employees as necessary. In some markets, the individual trainers were centrally located so that new employees from many stores could be trained as a group. The Vista curriculum for new employees when we visited included

- orientation (including a video and discussion of "This is CVS" and a segment on the manager's expectations and standards),
- a video and discussion on "Success Through Service,"
- a store tour,

- training on a terminal or register, and

- training on workstation appearance and upkeep.

Vista trainers delivered training in on-site facilities, from training rooms to break rooms depending on the store, and used demonstration cash registers and video equipment. This setup allowed the Vista trainers to shadow the new hires during their transitions from training to the floor to ensure that the new hires were comfortable with and capable of completing their job tasks.

Eventually, RLCs were introduced as new vehicles for providing training in the field. Their creation enabled the delivery of "mass" training within areas where CVS stores are concentrated. These centers, built primarily in metropolitan areas, were set up to handle all the training needs for all employees in the region, including new-employee orientation and training for photo lab operators and pharmacy technicians, as well as training for supervisors or managers. These centers were designed to allow individuals to receive training for their specific positions through classroom instruction, one-on-one instruction, computer-based training, and "hands on" learning.

In some cases, RLCs have partnered with government "one-stop" career centers that were created through the Workforce Investment Act (WIA) of 1998 to provide a range of necessary government services to welfare recipients, dislocated workers, unemployed individuals, and other disadvantaged populations. For example, CVS opened an RLC at the District of Columbia One-Stop Career Center in November 2000. By physically locating the RLC inside the same building as the government one-stop career center, CVS ensured itself more immediate access to unemployed workers seeking training and employment, and could also reduce the administrative hurdles for individuals hired through one of the government incentive programs. CVS is one of the first organizations in the country to take such a step.

The partnership with the center is not the only arrangement through which CVS worked with state and local government programs, but it does represent a model that CVS believes is successful. Thus, the organization is expanding its use of integrated RLC—one-stop career centers. Moreover, in many cases, because it will be used to provide qualified training for certain disadvantaged populations, much of the cost of the training provided at an RLC is reimbursed through government programs. This is true regardless of the fact that CVS is also permitted to use the RLC for training for other individuals unrelated to any government incentives.

As noted earlier, there are two specific lower-wage, entry-level positions for which there are more extensive training curricula available (beyond the training provided to most workers through the RLCs or the Vista training curriculum): pharmacy technicians[2] and photo lab operators. Both of these positions are important to CVS from a business perspective: pharmacy technicians can perform much of the work in the pharmacy, providing support to pharmacists who then have more time to carry out the duties requiring the attention of a licensed professional; photo lab operators provide enhanced service to repeat customers, producing a significant revenue stream. These positions represent primary targets for the placement of individuals through government programs because defined steps for advancement exist within them, a common requirement in many of the programs in order for the organization to qualify for incentives for such individuals. For example, within the pharmacy technician position, an extensive and well-defined series of training modules exists for moving an employee from an introductory level in pharmacy operations all the way up to becoming a nationally certified pharmacy technician. At the time of our study, approximately 10 percent of the employees in the pharmacy technician pipeline had come through various Welfare-to-Work partnerships.

Management Perspectives

The manager with whom we spoke in the downtown Boston store believed that the development of a central training site for entry-level workers had improved his store's operations in many ways. First, compared with the old system of training new employees when they were on the floor, most of Vista's training is carried out in a training room, break room, or other area out of the way of customers so that it is not as disruptive to store operations. Second, he saw advantages to having new employees understand early on their responsibilities as CVS employees. When they receive formal training on their first day on the job, they get an idea as to whether or not they will like their jobs. In an industry where it is not atypical for new hires to quit soon after starting, the formal training process provides a nice screening mechanism for the employees. Further, CVS data suggest that turnover in the Boston stores, while still much higher than is common in many other industries, has decreased significantly since the initiation of the centralized Vista program in this market.

While CVS sees the value in providing this new-hire training, and believes it is unique in the industry for doing so, there is little incentive to develop or provide training beyond the initial Vista program until a new employee shows an inclination to remain in a position for a substantial period of time. Training for specific functions or departments has usually been reserved for employees who have established at least six months of continued CVS employment. Because store managers must balance their budgets and achieve profits within an environment marked by constant turnover among front-line employees, it is difficult for them to devote resources to continuing education, and it is difficult for corporate offices to require that they do so.

The typical CVS store has been able to maintain a core group of long-term employees, while a large number of positions in each store are filled more than once throughout the course of a year. This appears to be a fairly rational approach; short-term workers typically do not view CVS as a career and, in turn, do not receive the investments that the organization might be willing to make for longer-term employees.

Management has been pleased with the outcomes of the training programs associated with government incentives. First, the Government Programs Department acts as a revenue center, not a cost center. By qualifying the organization for various publicly subsidized training partnerships or tax credits, this department has supported the need for training entry-level employees without burdening the organization with the various costs associated with such programs.

Further, CVS has found other, unexpected benefits through its participation in these programs. The employees who have come to CVS through government programs, particularly the Welfare-to-Work employees who were hired into pharmacy technician positions, have had lower rates of turnover and appear, according to managers, to take their jobs far more seriously and to display more commitment than their counterparts who were hired through traditional methods. In addition, the incentives created by the government programs prompted the organization to take actions that have resulted in better-defined, more efficient career tracks in the pharmacy and photo lab areas, enabling CVS to better develop the skills of workers in those positions.

Employee Perspectives

We spoke with six employees in the downtown Boston store, two of whom were students (one in high school, one in community college). The other four had been in the workforce for some time, and all had worked for other organizations besides CVS. Four were cashiers, one was a photo lab technician, and one was a pharmacy technician. The two students definitely viewed their jobs at CVS as temporary and were saving money and waiting for school to start again in the fall. Two of the employees who had worked in similar positions for other employers (a cashier and the photo lab technician) commented that the limited training they had received at CVS was much better and more thorough than that which they had received in other retail establishments. One cashier noted that she was hoping to move to full-time status soon in order to receive benefits.

The pharmacy technician noted that she had started in the store as a cashier, but after expressing interest in learning the pharmacy job, she was given the opportunity to do so. She progressed through much of the training track and was close to taking her certificate exam to become a certified pharmacy technician.

Overall, the employees were positive about the training they had received to do their jobs, and expressed no wish that CVS had provided them with more education or training opportunities.

LESSONS LEARNED

By both management and employee standards, CVS has done a fairly good job of orienting its entry-level employees to the basics of the company and their jobs. Although this training was fairly unremarkable, it was notable for its increasingly formal, systematic nature relative to training at many other retail chains. Management expressed some desire to be able to do some follow-up training with new hires after they had been working for a few months, but commented that it is hard to plan or justify such follow-ups when turnover is such an issue for the stores. This observation points to a fundamental factor that limits training for lower-wage workers: the high level of turnover for workers in that category.

Particularly notable at CVS were the career paths and specific training ladders that CVS created for the photo lab operator and pharmacy technician positions. Advantages seem evident for all parties— disadvantaged workers were trained for these jobs and developed new skills through funding provided by the public sector, while CVS was able to find new employees who proved to be eager to work and to continue working, again with the costs of such training subsidized by the government. What began as an effort to tap new sources of workers became an important factor in the development of new training paths at CVS, bringing about improved worker skills, improved retention, and what may prove to be windfall revenues for CVS.

In light of the strong economy present at the time of the case study, and as demonstrated by the success of CVS in this area, these publicly funded programs may represent fruitful paths for other organizations to explore in order to locate new pools of applicants to fill entry-level vacancies. This is especially true for organizations that can meet the requirement of providing well-defined paths of advancement for such individuals.

From a public policy perspective, it is instructive that the current structure of CVS's most extensive training initiative was developed partly as a response to existing government grants. Although CVS was clear about the human-resource–related benefits that have accrued to the organization and its employees from the new training initiative, it appeared likely that the program would not exist in its current form or scope if it had not been for the incentives provided by the availability of significant government grants.

Notes

1. Employment and sales figures taken from Hoover's Online at <http://www.hoovers.com>, March 2001.
2. What exactly does a pharmacy technician do? The answer: almost everything in the pharmacy except sign off that the correct medications and dosages have been prepared for the customer. Pharmacy technicians take prescription refill orders over the phone, enter them into the computer systems, take patient information

and record it, help with inventory of medications in the pharmacy, and help bottle medications for patients. With this position comes considerable responsibility, which is rewarded through higher pay. Frequently, the efficient running of the pharmacy is heavily dependent upon the pharmacy technician's skills and abilities.

In recent years, CVS has developed a training program for its pharmacy technicians to go through in order to become nationally certified pharmacy technicians. CVS's goal is to have all incumbent pharmacy technicians through the certification process over the next few years. Their reasons for doing this are twofold: 1) CVS has a commitment to providing real opportunities for significant development within this career track, and 2) CVS believes that it is in the organization's interest to promote the usefulness of voluntary industry standards, rather than tempting the federal government to increase its regulation of the chain-drug industry down the road. Since the prescription drug industry is under heavy scrutiny from federal regulators and others, the industry's primary players are holding themselves to strict standards in order to prove that further regulation is not necessary. In putting its pharmacy technicians through the certification program without that program's being required, CVS is trying to stay ahead of the certification game.

And what does national certification mean for a pharmacy technician? In 2000, the average certified lead technician at CVS earned around $25,000 per year. Through the process of becoming certified, the technicians also receive training, paid for by CVS, that provides them with highly transferable skills, including skills (such as those that are necessary only in hospital pharmacies) that are not applicable within CVS. In short, there are significant advantages to employees who successfully complete the pharmacy technician program at CVS.

7
Lacks Enterprises, Inc.

Lacks Enterprises, Inc. is a privately held, family-owned business headquartered in Grand Rapids, Michigan. Founded in 1965 as a die-casting company with fewer than 100 employees, Lacks has evolved into a world-class manufacturer of molded plastic components and systems for the automotive, computer, and telecommunications industries that at the time of our study employed more than 1,800 people.

As is the case throughout the manufacturing sector—but perhaps particularly for suppliers within the automotive industry—Lacks faces intensive pressure to improve product quality while cutting costs. At the same time, the Lacks production methods have become increasingly technologically complex, and the labor market has grown significantly tighter. As a result, Lacks faces a growing challenge in hiring the workers it needs to meet current and future growth requirements and the stringent quality and cost standards imposed by its customers.

THE WORKFORCE

Of the 1,800 employees at Lacks when we visited, approximately 1,400 were hourly. The profile of these individuals is fairly typical for a manufacturing setting. Almost all had completed high school (the exact percentage is unknown). Workers were predominantly white—as is the local population in the Grand Rapids area—although minorities were represented in ratios more or less according to their distribution in the overall population. About 60 percent of the hourly workforce was male. Newly hired workers have traditionally come from a variety of backgrounds, some arriving directly from school, others re-entering the labor force (for example, mothers who have been at home caring for their children), and others being veteran workers seeking new or improved opportunities.

Over the previous few years, however, to fill its needs for new workers, Lacks had increasingly come to rely on immigrants, many of whom had just recently arrived in the United States. In each of Lacks's 14 production facilities there were significant populations of foreign-born workers representing various countries, including Bosnia, Serbia, Mexico, Vietnam, Somalia, and the Sudan. Approximately 25 to 30 percent of Lacks's hourly workforce consisted of people for whom English was a second language; some spoke little or no English. This diversity obviously created organizational challenges from both operational and human resources standpoints.

Lacks competes for workers with many other manufacturing employers in the area. Consequently, Lacks must maintain a competitive wage level, since it is quite easy (particularly in a tight labor market) for people to move from one manufacturing firm to another. Entry-level wages during our study were $10 per hour, and experienced workers earned $12 to $13 per hour, depending on their jobs and the plants in which they worked. The benefit package, also critical to Lacks's ability to attract and retain workers, was also competitive with that of other employers in the area.

In the past, Lacks paid little attention to issues of recruiting and retaining hourly employees. Lacks's vice president for human resources told us that in the late 1980s, annual employee turnover was as high as 107 percent in one facility. Lacks's director of training quipped that the employment strategy was rather like "throwing mud at the wall; as long as there was plenty of mud, it didn't matter much if some didn't stick."[1] Several factors, however, had changed this view by the time of our visit:

- Most obviously, the labor market had grown significantly tighter.

- Lacks had come to realize that employee turnover was costly—in excess of $5,000 whenever a worker left after having been with Lacks for at least three months.

- Although it is difficult to assign a monetary cost, the disruption to productivity that results from such high turnover rates was very real.

- Lacks's technology was becoming increasingly complex. Consequently, more time was required before new workers became fully productive.

- Quality standards were becoming more demanding, which clearly created great difficulties when employee turnover rates were high.
- ISO 9000 standards required Lacks to focus more intently on individual worker training and, thus, worker retention.

EDUCATION AND TRAINING INITIATIVES

Taken together, the above factors led Lacks to change its philosophy toward its people. Once an environment characterized as "pretty autocratic," it had already evolved toward a more enlightened view with regard to human resource management.

As part of that evolution, Lacks established a formal training function in the early 1990s. Somewhat unusually, the training department's primary focus was on hourly workers and their training needs. Only after several years had the training department begun to turn its attention to the developmental needs of its salaried workforce.[2]

As in most manufacturing settings, most training for hourly workers was provided on the job. Lacks, however, by no means considered this to be "informal" training. In fact, an important part of Lacks's performance improvement strategy has been to "formalize" on-the-job training. It has done so in several ways, including:

- creating a network of "job skills trainers" within its hourly workforce; these individuals had been identified as exemplary workers, possessed superior people skills, and expressed a desire to train others;
- implementing a formal and extensive "train-the-trainer" program for these job skills trainers;
- paying these trainers an additional dollar per hour for time spent training other workers;
- focusing on formally analyzing production jobs, identifying the competencies that workers needed to do those jobs, and developing checklist systems to ensure that new workers acquired those competencies; and

- formalizing the process by which new employees became oriented to their jobs by assigning them to a trainer during their first few weeks on the job.

In addition to this formalized system of on-the-job training, Lacks also put unusual emphasis on other training for its hourly workforce. For example, in 1999 the hourly workforce received over 80 percent of all the hours of formal training delivered at Lacks (whereas management received only 20 percent of all formal training). Moreover, nearly half the time that hourly workers spent in formal training was on skills with a high degree of portability (such as problem solving and leadership skills), with the other half being devoted to job-specific, basic skills.

Lacks offered a wide array of classes to its hourly workforce, including English as a second language (ESL), basic computer skills, workplace mathematics, plastics technology, team skills, problem solving, leadership and supervision, and various safety and environmental training. The ESL classes were provided by local community education and public school systems with state funding. Lacks also benefited in recent years from several Michigan Economic Development Job Training Grants. The director of training estimated that they had been able to increase the level of training provided to the hourly workforce by 15 to 20 percent as a result of assistance from the state of Michigan.

Whenever workers were required to attend training classes, they were typically released from their regular jobs to do so and were paid at their regular hourly rates. If class attendance constituted overtime, then workers were paid overtime rates. In addition, although there was no guarantee, some supervisors attempted to provide time off for workers to take non-mandatory classes offered on site during regular working hours.

Lacks also had a tuition reimbursement plan that covered 75 percent of all tuition for approved courses, and offered bonuses to employees who completed degrees or certificates under the program. Participation in the program increased by about 30 percent between 1996 and 1999, doubtless because of the increased focus that was paid to learning by Lacks's mid-level managers.

Management Perspectives

Lacks management admitted that it was difficult (perhaps even impossible) to quantify all the benefits that resulted from the resources devoted to training its hourly workforce over the previous few years. But at one level, it could be argued that the very survival of the enterprise had depended, at least in part, on improving the ability of its workers to respond to customer demands for "faster, better, cheaper."

Another major and more readily quantifiable benefit that Lacks management assigned to the training for its hourly workforce was a significant reduction in employee turnover. Before its training program began, turnover at Lacks was typically slightly above that of other comparable employers in the Grand Rapids area, but by the time of our visit Lacks's turnover rate was about half that of its benchmarking group. Management attributed this decline in turnover largely to better worker education and more sophisticated human resources practices. And although no attempt was made to do a formal cost-benefit analysis, even the simplest calculations revealed that the benefits of training from reduced turnover alone were many multiples of its costs.

One frustration that both managers and employees face with regard to training is the difficulty of finding the time to do it. Production schedules are unforgiving—it is often impossible for people to leave their work stations to attend classes, even those offered on site. And the expense of paying workers to take classes after hours is prohibitive. It is interesting to note, however, that some managers at Lacks seemed to be either more willing or more able to arrange work schedules so that their employees could participate in the voluntary training opportunities.

Employee Perspectives

We found the employees at Lacks Enterprises to be very familiar with the on-the-job training programs, the on-site voluntary training programs, and the tuition reimbursement program. The voluntary training programs were not available to the most recently hired workers (those who had been with Lacks for less than three months), but since the newest workers had their hands full learning the basics of their jobs, the voluntary training, of necessity, had to wait until the new employees became proficient in their jobs.

Echoing managers' comments, workers reported considerable difficulty in getting released from work to attend the on-site elective courses; however, the extent to which workers felt that this significantly hindered their participation in training varied. Each worker had an individual development plan that outlined a course of learning. The extent to which these plans were actively supported seemed to be determined, in large part, by the enthusiasm and encouragement of that worker's supervisor.

In general, the workers with whom we spoke were positive about the learning opportunities that were available to them at Lacks. They had taken a wide variety of courses, ranging from basic math courses taught on site to technical courses taught at the local community college. They reported that the courses were typically well instructed and that they were able to learn a great deal. Several workers, however, did note that retaining the material covered in computer classes was difficult—if there was little or no opportunity to use that knowledge in their jobs, it quickly deteriorated.

A notable aspect of our interviews with workers was the degree to which they independently noted the effects of Lacks's training initiatives on the work environment. In particular, they noted that training had contributed to a noticeable reduction in turnover and that the ESL initiative had a positive effect on the work environment.

LESSONS LEARNED

Lacks was one of the two for-profit firms that we visited during the case-study phase of our research. Perhaps the most striking aspect of Lacks's approach to training for its hourly, primarily low-wage, workforce was the importance of management's mindset. It was not that Lacks spent an unusual amount on training in comparison with other manufacturing firms. In fact, Lacks spent less on formal training per employee than did other comparable firms. The difference was rather its intense focus on the hourly workforce. Lacks focused first on training programs for hourly workers because "these are the people who do the work"; training for management followed. In most firms, typically, the order is reversed.

Also striking was the extent to which training had been used as an integral component of a cultural shift. As production processes became more complex and, simultaneously, labor markets became tighter, the management at Lacks realized that their human resource management strategies had to change. Workers could no longer be treated as disposable, and the environment had to become one in which high-quality standards could be built in, rather than mandated.

As part of this shift, Lacks had, over the preceding several years, gradually developed a continuum of education and training interventions for its hourly workforce. At one end of the continuum was a structured orientation and on-the-job training program, complete with well-defined competencies and checklists to ensure that workers achieved the required level of competence. At the other end of the continuum was a formal education system that provided highly portable skills and knowledge (such as problem solving and leadership skills).

Hourly workers and management had both come to the same conclusion: that Lacks's investment in training had resulted in a more efficient production environment and a notable reduction in turnover. Although no attempt was made to assign a dollar value to these benefits, it was clear from discussions with management that the benefits significantly exceeded the costs that had been incurred in achieving them.

Like CVS, Lacks was resourceful in seeking out grants and finding assistance in its grant-writing activities. Being situated in the state of Michigan, which has made more of a commitment than most states to providing funds for workplace education, was an important factor in Lacks's learning initiatives for its hourly workforce. Lacks's training director estimated that the availability of these funds resulted in a 15 to 20 percent expansion in the number of hours of training that it could provide. And this funding was certainly an important enabler of Lacks's programs to provide instruction in English as a second language to the growing number of non-native speakers it employs. At Lacks as at CVS, the two for-profit firms we studied, the availability of external (publicly financed) incentives had a significant effect on the nature of training.

Finally, the role that individual managers and supervisors played in fostering the education and training initiatives at Lacks should not be underestimated. Some managers seemed to be willing to go out of their way to rearrange schedules so that workers could attend on-site training courses; others seemed less willing or able to do so. Finding ways to convince supervisors of the value of learning is almost certainly an important component of the success of such training programs.

Notes

1. This and other such quotes, both direct and indirect, are taken from our notes made during the various case study interviews.
2. As the evidence reviewed in Chapter 1 indicates, employees are more likely to receive workplace education and training if they are highly educated or highly paid. Consequently, Lacks's focus on providing training for its hourly workforce first was unusual.

8
LYNX—The Central Florida Regional Transportation Authority

The LYNX bus system is headquartered in Orlando, a city known for its standard-setting hospitality industry. Disney's presence has set an extremely high customer service benchmark for the area's other service providers. Despite its public nature, the LYNX bus system is no exception. A system that, when we visited, employed 480 bus operators and ran 56 routes across the tri-county area surrounding Orlando, LYNX had struggled to meet those high standards in the past. In the early 1990s, buses were not viewed as a desirable mode of transportation; they were unattractive and dirty. Typically, only the city's most disadvantaged people rode the bus. Regardless of its mission to serve the public using public funds, the organization had struggled to stay in the black, and knew that it must make improvements before things got worse.

Today, the bus company boasts having won the American Public Transit Association's Public Transportation Award in both 1996 and 1998 and continues to enjoy consistent increases in ridership. How did the organization make such a turnaround? Physical modifications to the bus fleet began the process. After an overwhelmingly positive public reaction to painting one bus "Pepto-Bismol pink," LYNX continued to clean up its fleet and paint the buses bright, eye-catching colors. At the same time, it adopted the LYNX name and a new logo, making the former Tri-County Transit (TCT) buses a lot easier to recognize and talk about. It also adjusted routes to make them more convenient to customers. All these changes helped improve the appeal of riding the bus and increased ridership. But the change that is believed by management to have made the most impact on LYNX's turnaround was the decision to implement a bus operator training program focused on customer service. This decision fundamentally changed the nature of the bus operator job. Instead of simply hiring drivers who had the necessary licenses, LYNX decided that it was important to hire drivers with the ability to be customer service representatives.

THE WORKFORCE

With the fleet of buses and schedule of routes it had at the time of our visit, LYNX could employ approximately 480 drivers. To cover the 56 routes throughout the Orlando metro area and to devote enough resources to rush hours, LYNX scheduled drivers for split shifts. For instance, a driver could work the morning and evening rush hours, with time off during the middle of the day when it was less busy. LYNX then was about 30 drivers short of a full staff, with overtime common. The tight labor market combined with competition from the Orlando area's theme parks, hauling companies, and various other organizations recruiting drivers all contributed to the shortage of workers and the need for overtime.

The workforce from which LYNX hired its bus operators was not unlike those in metropolitan areas throughout the country. Several factors, however, made LYNX's recent history stand out within this tight labor market. First, when LYNX changed its image and began its intense focus on customer service, the company realized that in order to best serve its customers, it needed to hire employees who were not just drivers but who could also fill the role of customer service representatives. LYNX implemented a training program focused on customer service for its incumbent drivers (as discussed below), and it relied on attrition and turnover to replace the operators who could not meet this new standard of customer service.

In short, the company decided that it took more than being a good bus driver to be a good LYNX driver. Thus, LYNX hired many operators who were not certified or licensed bus operators, but who showed promise of possessing a "LYNX-like" attitude. The 1992 mission statement stated: "The LYNX mission is to create and provide a comprehensive transportation system for residents and visitors to Central Florida that offers quality customer service in a cost-effective manner" (Central Florida Regional Transportation Authority 2000). In fact, LYNX became one of the few bus companies in the country that would hire people from outside the industry and then provide the training necessary for those new hires to get their licenses. Focusing its hiring practices on the skill sets associated with customer service, rather than with operating a bus, changed the pool from which LYNX hired its operators and showed where its priorities lay.

The second way in which LYNX adapted to the tight labor market was by putting less emphasis on the scores from the customer service aptitude entrance test given to job applicants. When the testing process was first put into place, LYNX accepted applicants based on an average score of 70 percent or higher. However, the labor market forced it to relax the entrance requirements, depending less on exam scores to determine whom to interview. This had the effect of bringing a larger pool of potential drivers into the training process and at the same time widened the range of aptitudes and abilities to be found among a training class. The training function thus became more of a screen for good employees than it had been in the past. Although this change did not alter the basic training function, it placed more responsibility on the training department to evaluate the abilities of trainees and to decide whether or not they had the skills and attitudes to become LYNX bus operators.

EDUCATION AND TRAINING INITIATIVES

At the time of our visit each new class typically had six to eight students who went through seven weeks of training together. The number of routes LYNX covered—56 routes with over 5,000 stops—determined the length of this training, and each person was trained on all routes. During the first five weeks, LYNX's five training instructors conducted a course certified by the Transportation Safety Institute in a multimedia-enhanced classroom environment. They spent two hours each day in the classroom covering driving skills, bus operations, safety, route maps, and driver review sheets. Then, instructors and drivers moved out to buses (carrying no passengers), and the students took turns driving routes while the other students made notes and asked questions of the instructor. This process forced the students to review techniques and information covered in the classroom and to apply those skills in a driving environment.

During the last two weeks of training, new drivers were placed with line operator instructors for on-the-job training. The 49 line instructors were experienced drivers who received an extra 50 cents per hour while they trained a student. No official training or certification was required of the line instructors other than that they must have been LYNX bus operators for at least one year.

In the sixth week, each new employee was assigned to one instructor on one route to focus on fare box operations and customer relations face-to-face with the public. During the seventh week, each student was placed on a different route with a different instructor each day. This process alleviates any anxieties new hires might have had about being placed on new routes when they were needed to fill a vacant shift temporarily.

At the end of the official training period, each new driver was assigned a mentor. The mentors were senior operators who had applied to become mentors and who had been screened for their performance records and their LYNX-like attitudes. The mentor program was implemented to address the problem of attrition of new operators by providing them with a confidant of sorts. LYNX believed that giving its new hires a "buddy" or pool of buddies who could answer questions and offer advice would improve employee retention. Although mentors received no additional pay for their role, they were involved in the implementation of the program, updated frequently on the program's progress, and included in decision making in order to help the program succeed.

Throughout their careers at LYNX, employees took part in safety and diversity training. In addition to the new hire training, other courses helped LYNX employees enhance or acquire new customer service skills. For example, LYNX purchased from the Canadian Urban Transit Association the Transit Ambassador program, which focuses on customer relations. The program, based on the principle that there are external and internal customers, conveys a value-added service approach to being a bus operator. All operators had to complete this training after one year of employment. The program is divided into one classroom segment per week for six weeks, giving the operators time between lessons to go back to their routes and apply the knowledge that they have gained. The topics covered in the Transit Ambassador program are fundamentals of the program, communication, special needs, complaints as opportunities, handling difficult situations, and stress management.

Management Perspectives

If management had not led the transformation of LYNX through a focus on customer service training, LYNX would be a very different place today. While it has been difficult to measure and quantify the effects of this new focus, LYNX can say that its ridership increased from 8.1 million in fiscal year 1991 to 20.7 million in 1999, that customer complaints declined with the use of the Transit Ambassador program, and that in a 1998 market study 85 percent of customers were very pleased with the service they received from LYNX. According to another market survey, name recognition has skyrocketed since the name change in 1993. These changes contributed to an environment in which LYNX was no longer concerned with dedicating resources to developing its image within the community; it knew it could continue to focus on the quality of service it offered the Orlando public and visitors.

Despite this dedication, however, the tight labor market and resulting bus operator vacancies made it difficult to deliver training to all of LYNX's operators, since LYNX had to keep a sufficient number of operators on the job. Management found that graduation rates from the seven-week training program for new hires declined slightly, and that it became more difficult to find people who possessed both operator skills and the required customer service attitude. Despite company recognition of the value of continuous training in terms of conveying to employees that they were important contributors to the success of LYNX, the Transit Ambassador program had to be cut for lack of operator availability for training. It was later reinstated for small groups of employees, but it remained extremely difficult to pull operators from their routes to attend training. Indeed, the direct tie between the numbers of front-line employees and the ability of the business to serve its customers 365 days a year proved an obstacle to training the entire workforce.

Employee Perspectives

Employees voiced mixed impressions of the training regime. Some operators thought that the initial training program was too long, especially for people who had previous experience driving buses. Some also voiced frustration with respect to the customer service training. Citing cases in which operators had to handle situations according to their own street instincts and using techniques with which they were personably comfortable, some drivers felt that some of the time spent on customer service training (the Transit Ambassador program) went beyond the necessary. Other drivers, however, were very happy with the thoroughness of the initial training, especially those who were new to the public transportation industry. The hands-on component of the initial training program received praise, as did the mentor and Transit Ambassador programs for allowing drivers to share their experiences with one another. Interestingly, some operators noted that the Transit Ambassador program provided learning that had value in their family lives as well as their work lives. Most employees talked about the importance of a top-down, management buy-in to customer service attitudes. They noted that observable customer satisfaction gave them momentum to continue doing their jobs well, and emphasized that continuous supervisor promotion and exemplifying of the LYNX-like attitude were integral to meeting that objective.

LESSONS LEARNED

Local public transportation authorities do not compete with one another for riders or revenues. As a result, information and best practices are shared among the members of the industry. LYNX uses training programs from Canada and Seattle. This sharing of information across the industry, especially with regard to training, has undeniably helped LYNX to improve its business. In the eyes of management, LYNX's focus on customer service, and the training programs that have supported that focus, have been central to the successful turnaround of the organization. Although it is difficult to isolate and quantify the financial impact of training, LYNX's management attributes a significant portion of the increases in ridership and customer satisfaction that it has enjoyed to the cultivation of the LYNX-like attitudes that training has fostered.

An important factor contributing to the impact of this training was the support of senior management and the enthusiasm of the training staff. While they struggled with the added responsibilities of screening that the training department took on in light of the relaxed entrance requirements, they felt that they were getting employees who were better suited for a customer–service–oriented environment by focusing from the start on the importance of training.

Such enthusiasm was not universal, however. Operators' responses were mixed—pockets of both enthusiasm and disenchantment existed among them. Some employees were enthusiastic about the LYNX-like attitude and the accompanying training programs, and reported that those programs created benefits for their home lives as well as their work lives. Other operators, however, reported that they would be content to rely on their own street smarts when interacting with customers, and not have to go through all the required training that LYNX instituted.

Those mixed attitudes have brought LYNX to its latest struggle—that of trying to sustain the LYNX customer service philosophy and the training programs associated with it. The struggle has been compounded by the tight labor market, which has created a shortage of operators. Moreover, there is the fundamental dilemma of training in a service organization. To implement training, workers must be taken away from their jobs. And when workers are away from their jobs, customer satisfaction is compromised—at least in the short run.

9

Two Medical Centers

Mary Greeley Medical Center
and UPMC-Passavant

Because of the similar challenges—both external and internal—faced by the two medical centers included in the case studies, we discuss them together in this chapter.

The Mary Greeley Medical Center (MGMC) is located in Ames, Iowa, a small city, about 40 miles north of Des Moines, that is home to Iowa State University. At the time of our visit, employing approximately 1,400 workers (involved in a wide range of medical and other supporting activities) and operating 200 on-site patient beds, MGMC was the primary major medical center for 18 Iowa counties. Founded with a private grant in 1916, MGMC is owned by the city of Ames, although there is no direct financial relationship between the hospital and the city—the city provides no operating financial support and MGMC pays no taxes. The governing body of the medical center, the board of trustees, is publicly elected.

The University of Pittsburgh Medical Center at Passavant (UPMC-Passavant) is located about 10 miles north of downtown Pittsburgh, Pennsylvania, in the North Hills section of the city. It is one of 16 hospitals in the Pittsburgh area that are affiliated through the UPMC Health System. A nonprofit organization, it originated as a community-based hospital in the 1960s, paid for by area residents who saw a need for a local hospital and raised the necessary funds to attract another Pittsburgh-area hospital that was looking to relocate. Independent until 1998, it recently agreed to join the burgeoning UPMC system, and is one of the most financially successful affiliates in that system. When we visited it was similar in size to MGMC, with approximately 1,500 employees.

The challenges, large and small, faced by both MGMC and UPMC-Passavant are fairly similar (and fairly typical for major medical institutions). In many areas, these two institutions have made similar decisions and pursued comparable human resource and training strategies in their continuing quest to provide high-quality patient care. At the same time, there are some interesting, but subtle, differences between the two institutions in certain details and emphases.

Although the quality of patient care is the foremost consideration driving hospital decision making, many of the other specific challenges that these institutions face actually come from outside their organizations. They confront an environment that is increasingly regulated from numerous angles. They see decreasing reimbursements from public programs (such as Medicare) and insurance companies, and are experiencing increasing competition from other hospitals (in the case of MGMC, this includes competition from hospitals in Des Moines, which in previous years would have been too far away to be considered true competitors). At the same time, newer (and inevitably more expensive) technologies and equipment become available every day, forcing constant change in some areas of patient care, as well as a constant need for developing new skills. We observed that, like all employers, these institutions, though located in very different areas, both had to operate in a booming economy, in which the effects of low unemployment could be seen in the twin challenges of recruitment and retention of employees. Overall, the specifics of these external factors may change day to day and year to year, but their general existence is constant.

The Joint Commission on Accreditation of Healthcare Organizations (JCAHO) is perhaps the most significant external actor in shaping hospital operations. JCAHO, a commission that has become the *de facto* certification authority for most large hospitals and medical centers in the United States, thoroughly evaluates all aspects of an institution's operations (usually every three years), measuring them against preestablished benchmarks. In recent years, JCAHO has expanded its attention beyond clinical functions in determining an institution's performance. Thus, hospitals must meet numerous JCAHO requirements, and training frequently plays a central role in meeting them (MGMC, for example, estimated that 90 percent of its training was directed to meeting regulatory requirements).

Both organizations were striving to ensure that, in the face of these many (and competing) forces, their ultimate goal—the provision of quality patient care—did not get lost in the thicket of these multiple other demands.

For example, UPMC-Passavant had created a number of specific initiatives that emphasized the centrality of patient care. The institution conducted sophisticated tracking of patient satisfaction and released monthly satisfaction reports to all staff, including some data specific to nursing units. Those reports, along with comparative data from similar-sized institutions, were shared with all staff. A hospital-wide customer service initiative to ensure "five-star service" by its employees was a top priority of the organization.

Indeed, management at UPMC-Passavant applied this patient care emphasis broadly, using it as the philosophical foundation for their approach to human resources and training. They believed that this emphasis reflected the hospital's position as a nonprofit, service-based institution that was truly owned by its surrounding community. The relationship with the surrounding community dates back to the circumstances surrounding the hospital's move into the North Hills area in the 1960s, a move that had been initiated by individuals in the neighborhood itself. Management reported that the original leadership of the institution made a conscious decision to emphasize its role in the community in order to keep its patients "from turning into numbers." The leadership of UPMC-Passavant has continued to espouse this perspective, deliberately applying it not only to patients but also to employees, viewing its methods of patient treatment as models for employee treatment as well, including making available individual development opportunities for all. It is noteworthy that this rhetoric was expressed not only by the management team, but also by many of the lower-wage workers interviewed, who saw this organizational commitment as an important factor in shaping the hospital's character on a day-to-day basis: "Everyone treats you like you're important and they want you to be here."[1]

Leadership was cited as a key source of the commitment to broad development opportunities at MGMC as well. Its focus was somewhat different, although the results from the perspective of lower-wage workers seemed strikingly similar. While UPMC-Passavant took a consciously philosophical approach, MGMC management downplayed the philosophy, focusing more heavily on factors such as regulatory requirements and simply ensuring that each employee was able to get the job done properly. Still, reflecting the views of its leadership, MGMC took an expansive view of what was necessary for each employee to know in order to actually get the job done. MGMC believed that successful employees needed not only job-specific understanding but also consistent access to a broad range of information on the medical field and the organization itself, including its technology and details in areas such as its current financial status. Even skills that enabled employees to improve their personal lives, such as financial planning, had been added to the mix. Despite some differences in emphasis between the two institutions, the result from the perspective of lower-wage workers was almost identical: Typical comments at MGMC were, "They show an interest in each person and give them an opportunity to learn," and "It's almost like a second family here."

THE WORKFORCES

The workers at UPMC-Passavant and MGMC had an extremely broad range of responsibilities, both clinical and nonclinical. A significant percentage of them—about 25 percent of the workers at each institution—earned less than $10 per hour. These lower-wage employees held various positions, as nurse assistants, switchboard operators, food service employees, office assistants, and child care workers. A significant (and growing) percentage of entry-level workers lacked sufficient work experience in their specific areas of employment, and therefore training was often required for new workers in order to ensure that they were able to develop the necessary skills and competencies to perform their jobs.

Both institutions confronted the common workforce-related challenges of the day, including increased turnover and difficulty in filling key positions. There was mounting concern regarding the problem of high turnover due in large part to the remarkably low unemployment rate prevailing in both communities.[2] MGMC had identified turnover as a key issue with its managers, and included it as a component of their reviews. Turnover was higher than the historical average at both organizations in 1999 (19 percent at UPMC-Passavant; 21 percent at MGMC), and both reported that a growing number of departing employees were leaving in order to earn more money elsewhere. Nevertheless, UPMC-Passavant continued to enjoy a slightly lower turnover rate than most of its sister organizations in the UPMC system. Average tenure among employees was approximately 15 years, indicating that many employees still were staying at UPMC-Passavant for much of their working lives.

At both institutions, the turnover rate was significantly higher among entry-level workers and those earning less than $10 per hour. UPMC-Passavant reported a particular problem in turnover among those holding part-time jobs. Although the administration had tried to reduce the number of part-time jobs in an effort to reduce turnover, the scheduling requirements in medical facilities made it difficult to reduce the percentage of part-time positions below a certain level.

Overall, therefore, the key concerns of both organizations with regard to their lower-wage employees were no surprise: they involved skill development, recruitment, and retention. As discussed below, both used their training programs—in somewhat different ways—as a key strategy in addressing all these issues.

EDUCATION AND TRAINING INITIATIVES

UPMC-Passavant employed 8.5 full-time equivalents in its education department, and this staff handled almost all training needs in the organization, with the exception of information technology (IT) training (most of which was outsourced). Unlike at many other hospitals, continuing medical education for doctors was not separated or outsourced at UPMC-Passavant; instead, it was included in the institution's training program, and often drew attendance from other area hospitals as well. In addition, the training staff was responsible for detailed training record-keeping, a time-consuming task that is important in providing the necessary documentation for external certification requirements and salary reviews. Earlier, the training program had been focused almost exclusively on training for the nursing staff. As part of an organizational re-engineering initiative in the mid 1990s, the education department's mission was expanded to include all the training in the organization. This change greatly increased the department's responsibilities in an effort to increase the overall effectiveness of training in the organization. By all available accounts (internal and external), the department had handled these added responsibilities with distinction, even winning commendation from various accreditation bodies.

At MGMC, a similar structure prevailed. The training staff included four full-time and three part-time employees, who handled most training needs in the organization, although training responsibilities were somewhat more decentralized to individual departments than they were at UPMC-Passavant. Some years ago, MGMC had decided to combine its nursing and nonnursing educational functions into one department. Record-keeping and tracking of training were central roles of this department, with such data used both to meet certification requirements and to provide information necessary for salary reviews. MGMC reported that its training budget had declined slightly in recent years, with management attributing this decline to increases in efficiency.

MGMC used an internally developed computer system to track job requirements and competencies as well as the specific training received by each staff member. Training staff time was estimated to be divided fairly evenly between clinical and nonclinical training. One centerpiece of the training at MGMC was an intensive, multiday orientation session required of all new employees. This began with a standard first day, for all new employees, to address organizational mission and integrity, quality assurance, safety, infection control, back safety, diversity, and other organizational logistics and basics. Additional training days followed in which content was tailored by department.

JCAHO has specific requirements for hospitals and their staff, and these requirements must be taken into consideration in determining training content and priorities. In recent years, JCAHO competency requirements have been expanded beyond the clinical realm (where they had previously been concentrated). As a result, hospitals are required to develop defined skills and competencies for workers at all levels of the organization, and to assess the competencies of all employees.

At both MGMC and UPMC-Passavant, which had previously extended training opportunities to all employees, these new JCAHO requirements served generally to complement the changes they had already implemented. Although the specific training content at both institutions varied widely depending on the department and job, most training offered fell into at least one of three (partly overlapping) categories: 1) training required to meet JCAHO (or other externally imposed) competency requirements; 2) training to meet specific needs identified by a given department (such as new technologies and procedures); and 3) education for a new employee, including both general orientation and the skills and competencies necessary for a particular job. Both institutions offered a wide variety of courses that were unrelated to any external requirements, including courses related to the health care field and others unrelated to the industry in areas such as personal development. The existence of these courses reflected the conscious commitment of the leadership of both institutions to make a significant variety of opportunities available to their staffs at all levels and in all departments.

Further expanding the range of opportunities, all the courses offered by the education department at UPMC-Passavant and most offered at MGMC were open to all staff members from any department in the institution. Education staff reported a somewhat unexpected benefit from this policy—many employees taking a class voluntarily treated it more seriously than did the participants for whom it was required, taking notes, asking questions, and otherwise exerting a positive influence on the class.

Among the most popular voluntary course offerings at MGMC were courses in areas of computer skills (including basic overviews of computers and operating systems such as Windows, as well as different levels of courses in applications such as Microsoft Word and Excel). At almost every organization we visited, in fact, computer skills were at the top of employees' lists of voluntary courses that they would like to be able to take. Although most organizations offered limited opportunities, at best, in this area, MGMC's small training staff included one full-time educator dedicated to computer training, the subject of the most popular voluntary courses offered at MGMC.

Reflecting their unusual commitment to making training broadly available, both organizations provided data indicating that in 1998, 100 percent of all their employees received some form of training. For comparison, among all organizations in the United States from which ASTD has collected similar data, the average is 77 percent; among other hospitals included in the ASTD database, the average is 86 percent. The two organizations addressed their training needs with fairly similar delivery strategies. At UPMC-Passavant, all formal training (required and voluntary) was typically delivered either through traditional classroom instruction or through the use of various self-learning modules such as videos or workbooks. Employees were paid for their self-study time for required training. The classroom training was described by more than one lower-wage employee as fairly intensive, with one commenting that it was far more advanced than similar training that he had received when employed at another hospital in the city. The education department at UPMC-Passavant was beginning to use learning technologies more extensively for some forms of training, but had been slowed, in part, by limited computer access for some staff. Much of the other training (particularly for new employees) was offered through structured on-the-job training, in which the new employee was often assigned to a more experienced employee within the appropriate department. That employee acted as a mentor, assessing the new employee's educational needs, and demonstrating how to use various machines, procedures, and so on, while monitoring the development of competency.

MGMC also delivered much of its training through the classroom, but reported a greater reliance on self-study (especially using workbooks) as a alternative method of delivering the required training. Its training staff had developed self-study versions of most required training courses, recognizing the need to make training available when it was convenient for participants. Indeed, it estimated that 30 percent of all new employees took the entire orientation battery of courses through self-study, with the requirement that they had to demonstrate the skills upon completion. Employees were paid for their self-study time for required courses. Although computers were not used to deliver non-computer-related training, that was one of the training department's priorities for the future (in the hope of retaining time flexibility while making some content more interesting than it was through workbook self-study).

At both organizations, individual evaluations and pay increases for employees were affected by an employee's participation in *required* training. MGMC reported that this had been a great incentive in helping to ensure compliance with training requirements. UPMC-Passavant withheld pay increases until an employee's required education was complete. It, however, also considered *voluntary* education in employee evaluations and merit-based pay increases that were above the norm; participation in voluntary training was viewed as evidence of an employee's commitment and willingness to go above and beyond the requirements.

Management Perspectives

One primary area in which UPMC-Passavant and MGMC differed from many other medical institutions with similar needs and requirements was the commitment of both institutions to a broad range of development opportunities for all staff, beyond simply the training made necessary by external (and other) requirements. As discussed above, the respective management teams at these two institutions described their motivations for providing such opportunities in qualitative terms that differed a bit in emphasis. At UPMC-Passavant, upper-level management viewed education as an integral component of the organization's dual (and related) commitments to its patients and to its employees. It was necessary to ensure that employees had the skills required to provide the highest possible level of care to the patients they treated, and education was an instrument for achieving that goal. Furthermore, they had come to recognize that the quality of the learning opportunities offered at UPMC-Passavant represented an important tool in attracting and retaining employees, a perspective confirmed in our interviews with lower-wage workers.

Although UPMC-Passavant management clearly recognized a link between the treatment of their employees and the treatment of patients, it was interesting to note that this management team also made what was clearly, at its heart, a purely philosophically driven case for employee education—they provided significant development opportunities to all employees simply because it was the right thing for their organization to do. The vice president in charge of human resources noted that one key factor that made this philosophy more possible at UPMC-Passavant, a not-for-profit institution, was the multiple-focus commitment to patient care excellence, employee satisfaction, and financial viability. Decisions were not driven solely by the bottom line.

At MGMC, the philosophical case was less important than the practical one—simply, a conviction that well-trained and broadly informed employees would be able to provide better patient care and would, moreover, improve the institution as a whole, making it a better place not only for patients, but also for employees. Management expressed the strong belief that education and development are particularly important in determining whether health care organizations will be able to survive. Addressing the need to attract new workers, MGMC management noted that they made little effort to highlight the range of development opportunities, but focused on a broader message about the entire benefits package at MGMC, with the consistent availability of training and other opportunities only a small piece of that message. Nevertheless, they believed that most new workers (many of whom had been attracted by word of mouth) were aware of MGMC's reputation as a good place to work, where advancement was possible (reflecting both the commitment to hiring from within, as well as any training development opportunities).

Despite strong advocacy from the organizations' leadership for the importance of broad development opportunities, neither institution was immune from the common problem of finding available time in the workday during which busy employees could receive training, both required and voluntary. This problem is exacerbated in a place like a hospital, since the workday can span any of the three separate shifts that run 24 hours a day. Both organizations reported that most departmental managers increasingly had come to recognize the importance, as well as the benefits, of the training offered. Most, therefore, worked closely with the education department in order to identify convenient times and locations to offer the required training to staff.

The education staff at UPMC-Passavant attacked this scheduling problem aggressively in other ways. They marketed themselves to all shifts, conducting surveys to determine what times and places were most convenient for training sessions. To make it as easy as possible for staff to participate, they made a point of being available and offering training in different department sites, during times outside the traditional hours, or for short sessions (no more than 30 minutes at a time). Overall, these approaches increased the percentage of required training that could be made available to staff in a classroom setting, without resorting to self-study methods. There was a much smaller impact, however, on the availability of staff to participate in voluntary training, the benefits of which were often less clear to departmental managers who were, therefore, less likely to approve participation in such courses during work hours.

At MGMC, finding time for employees to participate in voluntary training (including classroom training), although still certainly difficult for employees and trainers, seemed perhaps less problematic than at any other organization that we visited. Despite the usual requirement for individual managers to approve voluntary training before it was taken, most employees reported less difficulty than those at other organizations in getting approval and then finding the necessary time to participate in such training. It was difficult to pinpoint the explanation for this. Again, it is likely that it was driven by leadership, since the MGMC leadership emphasized the need, not just for development opportunities, but for *consistently available* opportunities. Thus, the concept of access was built into the organization's very definition of opportunity. Perhaps another explanation is MGMC's wide use of self-study as an acceptable form of training, which may have enhanced the capacity of the training staff to be flexible in offering voluntary courses at convenient times. Finally, an answer may be MGMC's unusually high number of offerings in the content area in which employees at all organizations expressed the most interest—computer training. Perhaps employees are more motivated to pursue voluntary opportunities and overcome logistical obstacles when they find them to be of significant interest.

The two organizations diverged in their approach to another aspect of development opportunities for employees: tuition reimbursement programs. MGMC had a fairly standard tuition reimbursement policy, in which up to $1,500 per year was available to all full-time employees who had been employed at MGMC for at least six months (a $750 benefit was available for "regular" part-time employees, who worked at least 20 hours per week). This was viewed by management as a standard element of the organization's benefits package.

UPMC-Passavant previously had decided not to offer a tuition reimbursement program, a common staple in most organizations (such a program is offered at 94 percent of all organizations surveyed by ASTD, and 93 percent of all hospitals). Management explained this as a conscious decision, made in order 1) to spread scarce training dollars as broadly as possible, rather than concentrating them on only those who chose to (or were able to) attend higher education classes, and 2) to ensure that the organization was able to recognize a more immediate impact from all its training expenditures. UPMC-Passavant did, however, have a benefit negotiated with nearby LaRoche College to offer significantly lower tuition for hospital employees taking classes there, and UPMC-Passavant had recently decided to implement a tuition reimbursement plan starting in 2001, believing that such a plan was a necessary component of providing a competitive benefits package for employees.

Overall, both organizations exhibited clear management commitment to providing training for the entire workforce, including lower-wage employees. Their slightly different approaches in some areas illustrate the common trade-offs that must be addressed by education departments in all organizations that provide broad training opportunities. Inevitably (and hardly unexpectedly) resources are limited and organizations must make difficult decisions about how to use their scarce resources to best achieve their goals. UPMC-Passavant targeted its resources in a very focused way to ensure its capacity to deliver quality in-house training, in person if at all possible. MGMC made some of its resources available through tuition reimbursement for purposes that often would not have directly benefited the organization. They were also more willing to deliver training in a nonclassroom setting, a compromise that enhanced flexibility while perhaps reducing overall effectiveness relative to classroom training. Partly as a result, they may have had greater capacity to provide consistent access to training than most organizations.

Employee Perspectives

At both organizations, numerous lower-wage employees verified many of the comments from management and the education staff. For example, at UPMC-Passavant, management's emphasis on treating all employees with respect and as valued members of the organization was validated consistently. "You're not just a body here," was one typical comment. Indeed, many of the lower-wage employees interviewed reported that they originally sought employment at UPMC-Passavant in part because of its reputation in Pittsburgh as a good place to work.

Most also reported that they expected to stay at UPMC-Passavant for a long time to come, generally for the same reason. Similarly, many MGMC employees described the hospital as a "great place to work" with a "fun environment." Many had sought employment at MGMC for just those reasons, and reported that they envisioned staying for the long term.

When asked for reasons why they expected to stay, employees at both organizations indicated that the development opportunities provided by the organizations played a significant part in their satisfaction. At UPMC-Passavant, these opportunities manifested themselves in two related characteristics: first, the wide spectrum of training classes available, and second, the institution's openness to movement between departments and its commitment to hiring from within. One employee noted, upon beginning work at UPMC-Passavant, that "it's a pleasant surprise to find that you suddenly have a career path." Another commented, "Once you're in, you're in, and everybody will help you get to where you want to get." At MGMC, comments were similar. In particular, employees seemed quite pleased with the broad and "equal" access to training courses. Many employees reported that they had moved among departments, viewing this as another significant benefit to working at MGMC.

Required courses received favorable reviews, with lower-wage employees from several different departments commenting on the usefulness and high quality of the courses that were necessary for their department or role. At MGMC, employees compared the formal training programs with the on-the-job training that many departments depended on to provide the detailed skills that a new worker needed in a given position, with the on-the-job training drawing some complaints: "They shouldn't rely so heavily on OJT because it's disruptive to other employees." Employees at both organizations agreed that tying pay increases to participation in required training was a strong incentive to meet all educational requirements.

Reflecting one of the apparent strengths in the education and training programs at both organizations, the staff of the education departments received quite positive reviews. At UPMC-Passavant, many employees commented on the training department's good organization and flexibility, as well as on the quality of its offerings. The enthusiasm and hard work of the training staff were also highlighted. At

MGMC, employees singled out the willingness of the training staff to work with them one-on-one when requested. Notably, most employees interviewed had taken several computer courses, many during work hours, and they highlighted the high quality and usefulness of that training.

The difficulty of integrating voluntary training courses into their schedules was the predominant frustration voiced by the lower-wage employees at both organizations. At UPMC-Passavant, most employees seemed well informed on the various training opportunities available each month (indicating that the education department's marketing was generally successful in creating staff awareness), but most also indicated that they were usually *unable* to take advantage of training opportunities in which they would have liked to participate, often because of competing requirements for their work time. "I'm just too busy," was the common refrain from the employees. This was a common, but less prevalent, complaint among employees at MGMC as well. Nevertheless, many of those who complained at MGMC still listed voluntary courses that they had been able to take relatively recently. A number reported that their supervisors had been supportive and made it possible for them to attend voluntary classes (again, most were computer skills classes).

LESSONS LEARNED

First and foremost, both hospitals clearly demonstrated the importance of leadership in ensuring broad development opportunities for lower-wage workers. A commitment from management to such opportunities was clearly reflected in the priorities of both education departments, as well as in the overall character and environment of the organizations, from management to entry-level employees. In recent years, external requirements (in the form of JCAHO certification) had complemented the commitment from management, making it difficult to separate the effects of the two factors. It is clear, however, that both can strongly influence the breadth of training and the audience targeted.

The education and training practices of the two institutions showed that it is possible to offer broadly distributed developmental opportunities without a need to make any sort of special, dedicated effort to include lower-wage workers, a group that is often excluded from such opportunities in many other organizations. It is notable (at these institutions as well as several other workplaces included in the case studies) how infrequently management singled out lower-wage employees in our discussions on their training perspectives and strategies. Rather, they pursued a training strategy for the organization's workforce as a whole, with lower-wage workers treated as a part of that overall workforce.

Further, the experience of these organizations suggests that providing meaningful *voluntary* development opportunities to all staff need not create a new burden for education departments. Simply extending to all staff those course offerings that already exist (whether voluntary or mandatory) is a huge first step that creates significant new opportunities for employees with only a modest increase at most in the work required of the education department. What's more, UPMC-Passavant found that opening courses to all staff often resulted in an unexpected positive overall effect in the class.

The limits to providing meaningful training opportunities—even in a work environment that is extremely conducive to broad development opportunities—were also amply demonstrated in these two organizations. At UPMC-Passavant, despite leadership from the top and a caring attitude from most department managers, it was clear that the potential benefits of the voluntary training opportunities it offered remained largely untapped. Many more lower-wage employees were interested in pursuing training classes but unable to participate during work hours. The education department staff's persistence and willingness to work directly with departments paid off in removing many of the schedule-related obstacles to *required* training, but managers remained (understandably) reluctant to lose too much work time when it came to *voluntary* training. MGMC further demonstrated that it is often possible to overcome the scheduling problems that can prevent employees from taking full advantage of voluntary training opportunities.

At MGMC, the training department confronted a different scheduling problem—how to make *required* courses available to the right staff at the right times. They ultimately decided to create self-study paper versions of almost all courses, which improved availability but likely reduced participants' interest and engagement.

Overall, despite each institution's inability to perfectly conquer all the obstacles it confronted, both organizations demonstrated that it is possible to conquer most of them. This is perhaps the most fundamental lesson that can be drawn from our visits to Pennsylvania and Iowa. Providing significant education and training to all employees is not impossible, and it need not require huge amounts of money (both organizations spent less per employee than the average organization surveyed by ASTD, and MGMC training expenditures had been decreasing in recent years). As these hospitals demonstrated, broad opportunities can be provided through a combination of organizational leadership identifying training opportunities as a priority, and an education staff pursuing that goal with enthusiasm and flexibility.

Finally, it seems to us that, as with other not-for-profit organizations we visited, the not-for-profit status of UPMC-Passavant and MGMC likely contributed to their capacity to make unusually broad, enlightened commitments to their employees. Not-for-profit status can provide additional flexibility for an organization's leadership team as it attempts to balance the various needs of patients, employees, and the community with sound business decisions and fiscal responsibility.

Notes

1. This and other such quotes, both direct and indirect, are taken from our notes made during the various case study interviews.
2. According to the Bureau of Labor Statistics, unemployment was 1.4 percent in the Des Moines area and 4.2 percent in the Pittsburgh metropolitan area in July 2000.

10
Wyoming Student
Loan Corporation

The Wyoming Student Loan Corporation (WSLC), in Cheyenne, Wyoming, is a private nonprofit organization that was created at the request of the governor of Wyoming in 1980 to provide student loan and related financial aid services to students with some relationship to the state of Wyoming. There are similarly structured organizations in 21 other locations in the United States. Its purpose has remained the same throughout its 23-year history: "to be the best at enabling Wyoming students to finance and obtain higher education at the school of their choice" (WSLC 2000). As of July 2000, WSLC had 46 employees and student loan holdings of approximately $200 million, holdings that had doubled since 1995. In its 23-year history, WSLC has provided more than 60,000 loans to students and parents.

WSLC competes with several national organizations in the student loan business but, because of restrictions in its charter, competes for business only within the state of Wyoming itself (this does include individuals from Wyoming who attend school in another state, and individuals from outside the state who attend one of Wyoming's nine postsecondary educational institutions). Despite WSLC's rapid growth, at the time of our visit it was still quite small relative to the many giants of the student loan business. Nevertheless, management believed that its small size and its Wyoming niche actually conferred significant advantages. Management focused the organization's efforts on exploiting the advantages, primarily by providing high-quality, personal customer service. In its marketing materials, WSLC touts the tangible benefits of these advantages: during business hours, WSLC customers will always have a phone call answered by a customer service associate (rather than an automated answering system); and borrowers can be confident that their loans will stay with WSLC, an organization that "understands the unique needs of Wyoming families, the financial institutions which serve them, and the higher education community" (WSLC 2000).

The organization confronts various challenges that have implications for its training and learning strategies and processes. Despite the inherent advantage of working within the state, WSLC still must operate simultaneously in the broader financial arena, a space that has been marked recently by significant changes: rapid technology growth that has created new skill requirements; new student loan regulations and legislation that greatly affect the operation of the organization, increasing the need to develop new skills and knowledge within the WSLC workforce; and additional specific compliance requirements that WSLC must meet as a nonprofit corporation.

The organization has turned to training and learning as its first instruments for meeting many of these challenges, a perspective that consciously reflects the organization's mission, to invest in learning. Although WSLC has been heavily education-oriented since its creation (for example, a former CEO and chairman of the board had decreed that the organization would make available unlimited reimbursement for postsecondary education for all employees, a policy that has since been scaled back), it is only recently that the organization has expanded its view of the need for broad-based formal education and learning opportunities in the workplace itself. Thus, training at WSLC increasingly has come to be seen by the leadership as a primary internal manifestation of the organization's educational mission.

The foundations of this view are not just philosophical; they are also clearly driven by the business needs of the organization. While there is a clear belief among the leadership team at WSLC that broad learning opportunities should be made available to all employees simply because that is the right thing to do, especially for a learning-oriented organization, there also exists side by side with this belief a commitment to learning because it improves the financial bottom line. The impact of these dual drivers can be seen in many of the specific aspects of WSLC's approach to training, as described below.

THE WORKFORCE

WSLC is a small organization with, at the time of our visit, 46 employees divided into four broad groups based on their function in the organization (office support, customer service, marketing, and management). Two of these generally fell into the lower-wage category: office support staff started at approximately $8.50 per hour; customer service staff at approximately $9.50 per hour. About 60 percent of WSLC's employees worked in one of those two categories. All full-time employees were required to have at least a high school diploma or the equivalent. Like every other organization included in this project, WSLC had experienced the effects of the strong national economy of the preceding few years. It responded, in part, by continuing its general policy of trying to stay a step ahead in terms of the wages it paid. This slightly higher pay enabled WSLC to compete relatively successfully for entry-level employees with its local labor market competitors, including government agencies, banks, and one large corporation. (Despite its relatively small size, WSLC is fairly well known in the Cheyenne area, being, in fact, one of the larger employers in the small community.)

Further, management believed that it was now doing a better job than in previous years in hiring the right people for the right jobs (supporting this conclusion, the organization had had no involuntary terminations in the preceding year). Recently, the organization had supplemented its existing hiring procedures with pretests of prospective employees in areas like math, grammar, and the ability to use a keyboard.

As a relatively small organization, WSLC had only a small management layer; most of its managers were relatively young and expected to stay at the organization for some time. This has potentially significant implications for WSLC's goal of hiring quality individuals and providing them with good development opportunities, since the prospects for significant upward mobility inside the organization are quite limited. How, then, could it provide quality opportunities to its employees? It is on this question that the philosophical orientation of the leadership team can be seen clearly. Aware that well-trained employees with little room to move up are likely to take their skills to another organization, WSLC still had made the conscious decision that it would prefer to hire good people, train them, and lose them, than to settle for someone else.

Paradoxically, it appears that this willingness to equip employees with skills that they could use elsewhere has helped to keep employees at WSLC, at least for a time. The organization in recent years had relatively low turnover (the average rate of annual voluntary turnover over the two years before our visit was 16 percent, and the average involuntary turnover was 7 percent); it had even been selected for inclusion in a recent industry benchmarking study because of its low turnover. This outcome runs counter to the expectations that such employees would be lost, and also to the economic theory that holds that the provision of general skills training creates incentives for employees to leave. As we found with some other case-study firms, this WSLC experience suggests that there are additional dynamics at play—such as company philosophy—that lead firms to provide general training to employees.

EDUCATION AND TRAINING INITIATIVES

WSLC had increased its focus on the importance of training in recent years: before 1995 it relied on informal on-the-job training; in 1995 it began documentation of work processes by the human resources department; and in 1997 it hired its first professional development manager. Before that position was created, training in the organization had been one of the many responsibilities of the human resources department. It had typically been informal, on-the-job training, often without any predetermined curriculum. By the time of our visit, however, the professional development department included almost two full-time equivalents who planned, coordinated, and supported all the organization's training, and also provided much of the actual instruction.

All training at WSLC emphasized the concept of cross-training, to ensure that all employees would have a good understanding of all jobs in the organization. This concept reflects the organization's dual commitments to customer service and to broad employee learning opportunities. Cross-training improves customer service because it means that most customer service representatives, regardless of their specific focus, will have enough knowledge to address a caller's concern without having to pass the call on to others; one manager commented that it was expected that phone calls would not be transferred. Most employees would benefit from the full range of training content provided by

WSLC, including instruction in the general skill areas (such as software applications and marketing or sales skills) that would be applicable at many organizations outside of WSLC. One additional benefit of cross-training is that it keeps jobs more interesting for employees, enabling them to undertake a wider range of tasks and challenges on a day-to-day basis, as well as helping them to avoid the high stress or boredom that may accompany a particular role at various times of the year (because of the cyclical nature of the student loan business, much of which is tied closely to the academic calendar).

The core of WSLC's training today was an unusually intensive orientation session for new workers that lasted at least 20 full workdays, touching on almost every aspect of the organization and the financial world in which it operated. (For some employees, such as customer service associates focusing on repayment services, the full orientation lasted approximately 30 workdays.) That new orientation program had been greatly expanded from the one used just a few years previously, in which training lasted less than a week, and left newly hired customer service associates answering phones after only a few days on the job. Management had realized that significant benefits would accrue if new employees were provided with a good deal more background and information before they were asked to provide useful service to customers. Thus, topics in the new, expanded comprehensive orientation included human resources information, customer service, student loan process and procedures, repayment servicing, computer systems and applications, reports, and due diligence.

The new orientation was taught by various WSLC employees, including the two in the professional development department, department managers, and other employees. Employees were also included as instructors in order to ease the transition for the new employees from the somewhat isolating orientation sessions to the actual work environment, which required frequent interaction with other employees. WSLC was also working toward an expanded role for employees as instructors, in the belief that they were often the best-equipped individuals to describe the nuances or complexities in a given area in which they worked on a daily basis.

Given the small size of the organization's workforce, the orientation course was typically presented to a small group of new employees (the session that was in progress when we visited WSLC included only two new employees). One customer service manager noted that the orientation was in a "continuous state of improvement" based on suggestions from new employees after they finished the orientation, as well as from other employees.

In 1999, each incumbent worker at WSLC received an average of over 40 hours of training, suggesting clearly that orientation was not the only training provided. Extensive in-house training was required for workers organization-wide. Thus, if a lower-wage worker received training in a given area, the CEO typically got the same training, and vice versa. Recently, typical subjects had included leadership, customer service, regulatory information, interpersonal communication skills, team building, and marketing and sales training.

There were also opportunities for employees to receive voluntary training (usually off site through an external training provider). The professional development staff circulated information to employees on such opportunities (more than one employee confirmed the volume as "tons of flyers"), and often highlighted a specific course for one or more employees who had expressed interest in that area, even in areas not directly applicable to their day-to-day work. The budget provided for every employee to receive some voluntary training off site at least once a year, and the leadership strongly encouraged employees to take advantage of that opportunity, ensuring that time was made available. As a result, almost every employee participated in voluntary training each year.

The financial commitment to such an extensive training operation was substantial. Per-employee expenditures were more than double those in the average U.S. organization, regardless of industry. Measured as a percentage of payroll, the results were similar. Even more strikingly, the trainer-to-employee ratio was much higher than in most organizations.

Most training was delivered through traditional classroom methods, although the organization had recently begun experimenting with Web-based training in one area. A typical tuition reimbursement program was also in place, providing up to $500 per semester per employee in reimbursement. Comparative data suggest that employee use of this program was fairly typical for the financial industry, and a bit higher than overall averages.

Management Perspectives

As noted previously, management's perspective on training reflected two catalysts—a philosophical belief that WSLC should provide extensive, quality training to its entire staff, and a business-related belief that such training would improve organizational performance. Philosophically, the commitment to training is a broad one and reflects the organization's long-term overall perspective on learning. WSLC has been active in education-related affairs in the Cheyenne community throughout its history, adopting local schools and participating in Junior Achievement programs. The CEO (who had been at WSLC for 17 years and CEO for five) was the chairman of the state Workforce Development Council. Both he and the chief operations officer (COO) had come from education backgrounds, and both stated that they believed in the importance of extending learning and development opportunities whenever possible to people who would not normally have them. "As the leaders of the corporation, we have a passion for education," noted the CEO, who continued by explaining his belief that "the difference between careers and jobs is education."[1] They therefore believed that the organization had an obligation to provide all employees with the opportunity to craft careers for themselves. "Instead of looking and saying we can't afford this, we first said we *are* going to do this—then we asked how we're going to afford it," commented the COO.

Alongside this strong belief in the importance of providing opportunities to their employees, the leadership believed just as strongly that such opportunities made good business sense. Because WSLC was a service-oriented organization, its success would reflect the satisfaction of its customers (or lack thereof). For that reason, the leadership team believed that every possible effort should be made to boost the abilities of its employees to provide quality customer service. The extensive training program at WSLC reflected that belief. The CEO noted that he did not understand why every business would not have the same perspective and make the same business decision to increase value by investing heavily in the skills of its workers: "It just doesn't make economic sense to me not to be doing it."

In looking at the effects of training at WSLC from that business perspective, the management team strongly believed that the increased emphasis on training had improved business results, including the productivity of the organization. Since 1995, the number of employees had increased by less than 50 percent (from 32 to 46), while the organization's financial holdings had doubled. While some of that increased efficiency could be attributed to the benefits of economies of scale, the leadership believed that it also reflected improvements in employees' effectiveness, which they attributed to the increased focus on broad cross-training. They suggested that the financial growth rate had been driven also by the increased capacities of WSLC's employees. The CEO stated that in previous years, when they were hiring poorly—that is, hiring employees who lacked the necessary skills or were difficult to train—he knew that much business was lost because of poor customer service. The organization's solid customer satisfaction ratings, according to a recent independent survey, reflected the success of its emphasis on improving customer service.

The leadership team pointed also to qualitative outcomes, noting that along with increased training came increased employee expectations, with the results that "as our expectations of employees grow, their self-confidence, abilities, personal independence, and interdependence have really blossomed." They noted that educated employees were far more capable of taking an "invaluable fresh look" at organizational operations and that, after developing the necessary confidence, they would then come directly to the CEO and make useful suggestions for improvement.

It is almost impossible to separate and measure the exact effects of training on an organization's bottom line. Nevertheless, the evidence does point to a correlation between WSLC's recent expansion of its training effort and the exceptional business results that followed. Importantly, the leadership was convinced that such effects existed; that conviction in itself strongly shaped the overall organizational perspective on training. Managers and supervisors were supportive of training opportunities, both required and voluntary, and some even played key roles in finding appropriate voluntary training for their staff. Finding time for voluntary training, while still always a challenge, did not appear to be the obstacle that it is in many other organizations, a state of affairs that can almost certainly be attributed partly to the organization's philosophy and partly to the structure and nature of the work conducted by many of the organization's lower-wage workers.

Employee Perspectives

As at UPMC-Passavant, management at WSLC consciously went to great lengths to emphasize the value of each employee to the enterprise. And, as at UPMC-Passavant, we easily perceived the success of this management effort at WSLC when we spoke with a cross-section of its employees. "I don't think we'd enjoy our jobs as much if we weren't respected and listened to as much as we are," commented one employee. Many cited the examples set by the CEO and COO, who seemed universally admired by the entire staff. Both made multiple rounds through the office each morning to ensure that they could at least say hello to every employee every day. The employees cited numerous other ways in which the leadership demonstrated its belief in the value of each employee—through the open communications policy, the friendly atmosphere, the higher-than-average pay, the respect for employees' outside obligations, and the many opportunities available for training and learning.

Employees confirmed that participation in voluntary training was commonplace, even during work hours, and that there typically were no problems in receiving supervisory permission to get time off work for training. One noted that her supervisor had taken the initiative to enroll her in two seminars in an area in which she had expressed a particular interest, even though the seminars were during work hours and were in an area that was not directly related to her job requirements.

Many employees also noted the extensive scope of the internally provided required training. "It seems like we're always in training for something," was one typical comment. Another observed that the range of training available was sometimes even intimidating: "The training has provided me with so much knowledge; it's scary because you don't know what you're getting into, but they're so friendly about it."

Employees spoke highly of the organization, and many expressed an expectation that they would remain working at WSLC for a long time: "It's the best corporation I've ever worked for." "Oh yes, I'll definitely be here for a long time." Others, however, did indicate an awareness that the opportunities to move up the job ladder at WSLC were relatively limited, and suggested that that might lead them to seek other employment at some point in the future: "I'd like to stay, but if I don't get to advance here, I may be up for something else eventually." One employee described a desire to move into management at some point—at WSLC if possible, but somewhere else if that were not possible: "Once you get new horizons, you've got to take advantage of some of them." Others seemed to feel that, at least in the short term, horizontal movement within the organization would be sufficient to allow them to take on new challenges and enable them to develop new areas of expertise without the need to move upward on the job ladder.

As we saw at several other organizations that we visited, WSLC employees clearly internalized the mission and goals emphasized by management. One lower-wage employee commented, "We're here to invest in learning, and that includes investing in our employees' learning." Many others also emphasized the consistency of the organization's external mission and the way that mission was carried out inside the organization as well. Indeed, the employees clearly identified training and learning with the very core culture of the organization. One enthusiastic employee, asked to describe the organization broadly as a place to work, answered by focusing immediately on training, "I love the training; I love the challenges; I love the learning; and all you do here is learn, learn, learn."

LESSONS LEARNED

As a service-oriented organization, WSLC depends for its success, and even its very existence in a highly competitive marketplace, upon its ability to meet the needs of its customers. It has chosen to address that need through an intensive system of training and learning, to ensure that all customer service associates (and, indeed, all employees of the organization) were as well-equipped as possible to address customer queries and needs. Although little quantitative evidence was available, management was convinced that the training program it had recently enacted had primary responsibility for the improvements in customer satisfaction in the organization.

One interesting dynamic at WSLC was the relationship between its commitment to providing expensive and valuable training to all employees and its limited ability to provide upward job mobility within the organization itself. It appeared that the positive aspects of the organization's training opportunities and overall culture usually outweighed the negative effects of its small size and its entrenched management and supervisory team. Perhaps more than in the typical organization, WSLC's culture had enabled employees to continue to find new challenges even without moving up in the organization. In the longer term, however, most employees would not be able to realize significant pay increases without moving up, either at WSLC or, more likely, at another organization. It seemed likely, therefore, that more employees would at some point choose to take their new skills elsewhere. WSLC management had, of course, already consciously decided to risk losing good employees rather than cut back on the training that they believed to be central to the organization's success. Probably because of the many other positive elements of its culture, WSLC has not had to deal with the full effects of this risk. If employee turnover were to increase in the years ahead, however, the already substantial financial commitment to training at WSLC would likely have to grow. It will be interesting to see how this dynamic plays out in the coming years.

More broadly, in comparison with most of the other organizations we visited, WSLC reflected an interesting mix of motivations—its broad-based training opportunities were driven by business needs while they were simultaneously grounded in the strongly held philosophy of the organization's leadership. After speaking with the leadership team, we came away with a sense that *either* of those two factors would have been sufficient justification for much of the existing structure of training at WSLC. This combination of factors may help to explain WSLC's curious capacity to overcome many of the problems encountered by other organizations committed to providing broad training opportunities to their workforce (most notably, the problem of finding time for voluntary training during the workday).

Overall, the nature of WSLC's business was not inherently unique; numerous small organizations are involved in some way in a heavily regulated area of the financial sector. The unique features about WSLC were both the way it met the challenges of its business—through building a culture marked by respect for each employee, with a strong emphasis on learning—and the results it achieved. Yet it is not clear why that approach should be so unusual. Although some ingredients of the organization's culture are somewhat rare, they are by no means impossible to find or develop. Overall, they enabled WSLC to build an organization with low turnover (despite a structure that would have been expected to encourage turnover), high morale, and excellent business results (including improved efficiency, strong customer satisfaction, and impressive rates of growth)—a set of outcomes that would be more than satisfactory in almost any business setting.

Note

1. This and other such quotes, both direct and indirect, are taken from our notes made during the various case study interviews.

11
Case Studies

Lessons Learned

During the case studies, phase 3 of our research, we learned much about what motivates organizations to provide significant training opportunities to their lower-wage workers, what challenges they face in doing so, and what strategies they use. We had posed three questions: First, why provide training to lower-wage workers? Second, what are the barriers to providing training to lower-wage workers? And third, what strategies and activities are most effective in overcoming those barriers? In this chapter we discuss the lessons we learned in answer to those questions and also draw some general conclusions regarding the nature of employee demand for training.

WHY PROVIDE TRAINING TO LOWER-WAGE WORKERS?

We found that various factors shaped the decision by these organizations to make strong commitments to providing quality training opportunities to lower-wage workers. As noted above, our selection of the small group of case-study organizations from the 40 organizations included in the telephone survey phase of the study was based expressly on their high level of dedication to lower-wage worker training. As a result, we were not surprised to find that these organizations differed in some ways from the broader sample of telephone survey organizations. One difference that became evident was the set of factors that appeared to drive their training strategies for lower-wage workers.

The set of priorities that emerged for these organizations has some subtle differences from the larger sample. For example, philosophy was a key factor in a larger percentage of the case studies. At the same time, we also found more of a general bottom-line perspective, in which economic factors and nature-of-work factors worked together to drive training decisions, particularly for organizations in the services sector. And we found that specific external forces played a larger role for these organizations. These main categories of motivating factors are discussed in additional detail below.

Philosophy

A select few of the organizations we studied had made a commitment to training lower-wage workers because they felt it was the "right thing to do" from the perspective of both the workers and the employers. As an organization that is very conscious of its role in furthering the education of others, the Wyoming Student Loan Corporation (WSLC) made the education and training of all employees an organization-wide priority. Training has come to be seen by WSLC's leadership as an internal manifestation of the organization's educational mission.

Another organization that made a philosophical commitment to training is the University of Pittsburgh Medical Center (UPMC) at Passavant. In recent years, the leadership of this organization has adopted a number of initiatives to emphasize the centrality of patient care and satisfaction. As they have promoted this patient-care perspective, they have deliberately set out to apply it to employees as well, providing a broad range of learning and development opportunities for all staff, including lower-wage workers.

Bottom Line

Although a philosophical commitment to training for all employees may not be the norm among U.S. organizations, others have come to an improved understanding of the importance of training for lower-wage workers because of business goals and needs. In recent years, the tight labor market in the United States forced many organizations to take a hard look at improving their systems for recruiting, developing, and retaining quality employees. Others view training as a necessary investment in providing their existing workers with new competencies and new skills.

The importance of training as a bottom-line issue is perhaps most apparent in organizations with a service orientation. These are organizations where lower-wage employees regularly interact with and serve customers and where the quality of those customer interactions has an important impact on the bottom line.

UPMC-Passavant, as noted above, made training a central element of its campaign to improve patient satisfaction. Similarly, the Central Florida Regional Transportation Authority (more commonly known as LYNX) adopted a bus operator training program focusing on customer service as part of a broader (and very successful) effort to build ridership by improving the appeal of riding the bus.

Also looking to training as a way to improve customer service is the Boeing Employees' Credit Union (BECU). With approximately 63 percent of its staff in front-line positions, as tellers and call center customer service representatives, for example, BECU views training as a central element of its efforts to fulfill the traditional credit union philosophy of "people helping people." Of course, training at BECU and other service-oriented organizations achieves other business objectives as well. Indeed, in some regards, training functions as a form of fringe benefit. As BECU's director of training told us, "Tight labor market or not, the challenge to keep good employees and maintain low turnover exists."[1]

Indeed, overcoming the challenges of recruitment and retention is a principal factor in several of the case-study organizations' embrace of training. At manufacturer Lacks Enterprises, for example, employee turnover in recent years had reached as high as 107 percent. After the company came to grips with the real costs of turnover—more than $5,000 whenever a worker left after being with the company for at least three months—it established a formal training program that management credits with a substantial reduction in employee exits, due in part to improved worker education.

External Forces

Other organizations are embracing training for lower-wage workers not necessarily out of a sense of mission or to address internal business concerns but to respond to and, in some cases, appease outside forces. Among the organizations we studied, those forces included government programs that encourage organizations to provide career paths and training for these workers, as well as client demands that organizations and their workers abide by certain quality standards.

In addition to its philosophical commitment to education, for example, WSLC had very clear reasons to make broad learning opportunities available to all employees: new student loan regulations represented an external force that increased the need for new skills and knowledge among the WSLC workforce.

CVS Corporation provides another example of how government can play a role in spurring organizations to pay special attention to this issue. In recent years, the retail drug chain has established a Government Programs Department to coordinate its participation in a wide variety of federal, state, and local programs designed to promote career opportunities for former welfare recipients.

Today, this newly created department acts as a revenue center for the company, qualifying CVS for a variety of publicly subsidized training partnerships and tax credits. In some cases, CVS actually partners with publicly supported career centers to provide training to some new employees in the same locations where government provides other services to welfare recipients, unemployed individuals, and others.

For Lacks Enterprises, it was not government but customers that helped to focus the organization's attention on training for lower-wage workers. More specifically, customer demands that Lacks comply with the International Organization for Standardization's ISO 9000 standards forced the company to take a fresh look at how worker training could improve product quality.

External regulations are typically viewed as a burden by employer and employee alike. Such requirements can, however, greatly affect training practices in certain industries. In the health care field, for example, at both UPMC-Passavant and the Mary Greeley Medical Center (MGMC), an external accrediting body was an important outside influence as the organizations devoted new resources to training. New requirements from the Joint Commission on Accreditation of Healthcare Organizations (JCAHO) helped focus both organizations' attention on key employee and organizational performance issues. MGMC, in fact, now estimates that 90 percent of its training is aimed at meeting JCAHO's regulatory requirements.

The hospital examples—and Lacks, too—show how external forces are increasing the *demand* for training: regulatory and industry standards, as well as customer demands, essentially require that a company upgrade its worker skills and performance. At CVS, on the other hand, it is the *supply* of training that is affected by the outside forces—in that case, the government's interest in promoting more training opportunities for lower-wage workers.

WHAT ARE THE BARRIERS TO PROVIDING TRAINING TO LOWER-WAGE WORKERS?

Despite the varied motivations that support and validate an organization's adopting quality training initiatives for lower-wage workers, such workers generally receive far less training than higher-wage workers. Why is this? In the course of our case-study research, we identified four principal barriers that stand in the way of training lower-wage workers. Notably, these barriers affect lower-wage workers even in the case-study organizations, which are generally far more predisposed to providing such training than other organizations.

Nature of Work

More so than their counterparts at other wage levels, lower-wage workers generally spend all their working hours in one place, be it at a call center, an assembly line, or the wheel of a bus. Anything that takes these workers away from the physical location of the job site inevitably prevents them from doing their work. Moreover, the nature of their work does not allow deferring the work to a later time. Thus "nature of work" challenges deter organizations that might otherwise be interested in providing their workers with training and development opportunities. At BECU, for example, employees reported that the nature of some jobs—including tellers and call center representatives—made it difficult to schedule training. Similarly, at the manufacturer Lacks Enterprises, managers and employees alike noted that the requirements associated with the company's "unforgiving" production schedules could make it difficult for people to leave their work to attend classes.

Finding the time to train lower-wage workers is complicated by the fact that these workers often work in shift rotations. Because different people are working at different times, it becomes a real challenge to create accessible training opportunities for all. At the two medical centers we studied, for example, the typical employee "workday" could occur during any of three separate shifts that ran 24 hours a day. The challenges that lower-wage workers face in leaving the physical worksite to receive training suggest an opening for individualized computer or electronic "e-learning" strategies that would allow workers to build their knowledge and skills without having to attend traditional classes. But e-learning's potential in freeing workers to learn "anytime, anywhere" is far from realized; most case-study organizations reported that they were only now exploring the possibility of using learning technologies to deliver a significant portion of their training, or were just beginning to use them.

As a result of these challenges, organizations often are forced to choose between the immediate need of having employees on the job and the longer-term need of having them learn to do a better job. Not surprisingly, the immediate needs frequently take precedence.

Lack of Evidence of Effectiveness

Another major barrier that we identified is the absence of good evidence that investments in training for lower-wage workers pay off in increased effectiveness. There is no doubt that employers and employees alike would be more receptive to training if they had better information about how it would improve, on the one hand, the organization's bottom-line performance and, on the other, the individual's job and income prospects. While many people might intuitively understand that training is a worthwhile investment, the general lack of incontrovertible evidence of the link between learning and performance inevitably reduces training's appeal.

Thus executives and managers may be reluctant to invest in something with no certain payoff. And employees may not understand the benefits that can accrue to them as a result of training. Some LYNX employees, for example, expressed frustration about the organization's customer service training, saying that it went beyond the necessary and that bus drivers ought to be able to handle situations according to their own "street instincts."

Improving people's attitudes toward training—among both management and lower-wage employees—is an obvious first step toward increasing participation and support in organizational learning programs. But many people, it appears, will be reluctant to commit themselves fully until they better understand exactly what training can accomplish, both for themselves individually and for their organizations.

Conflict between Downsizing and Training

In the manufacturing sector in particular, an important and formidable barrier to the provision of training for lower-wage workers is the simple fact that many of these workers' jobs are on their way out. In today's hypercompetitive economy, many organizations are automating work in response to the relentless pressure to wring out costs of production. The result is an inevitable tension between a long-term strategy of downsizing and a short-term strategy of maximizing the productivity of the existing workforce.

At one manufacturing firm that we visited in the course of our research (the firm is *not* among those described in the seven detailed case studies), the vice president of manufacturing acknowledged this tension, saying that it had been very difficult for the organization to raise prices. The result, he said, is a push to use technology to reduce costs, a strategy that will drive out increasing numbers of entry-level jobs. At the same firm, a lower-wage worker confirmed that the downsizing strategy already was having an effect on the provision of training. Hired for an apprenticeship, she said that she had not received the exposure to a wide variety of positions that she had been promised. "The training is not getting provided because they don't want people to learn new things," she said. "They want people to leave."

High Turnover among Lower-Wage Workers

At CVS, management reported a reluctance to dedicate significant resources to training the majority of the company's lower-wage employees because most of its front-line workers left their jobs in a period of months, if not weeks. Although the company devoted considerable effort to training professional and managerial staff, most new employees hired off the street for "floor" jobs in CVS stores received only a basic orientation and training in the operation of cash registers. This reflects a fundamental hurdle that must be overcome in any initiatives to increase the training of lower-wage workers: in at least some situations, even firms that have displayed an attention to (and an awareness of) the benefits of training for some categories of lower-wage workers had determined that training cannot possibly be cost-effective for other categories of such workers.

WHAT STRATEGIES AND ACTIVITIES ARE MOST EFFECTIVE IN OVERCOMING THESE BARRIERS?

Some organizations are more successful than others in overcoming the barriers to providing high-quality training opportunities for lower-wage workers. What makes these organizations successful is their recognition that training is important to organizational and individual performance. Both intuitively and by observation, they understand that training has a clear impact on productivity, employee retention, and other performance measures, and they are willing to invest as necessary to make training for lower-wage workers an organization-wide priority.

Leadership Commitment

A top-down, leadership commitment to the value of learning opportunities for all workers is the principal characteristic that defines those organizations that are fully realizing training's potential. At the Wyoming Student Loan Corporation, there is a clear belief among the organization's leadership that broad learning opportunities should be made available to all employees, both because it is "the right thing to do" and because it improves the financial bottom line. Management's commitment to training stems in part from the fact that WSLC is a service-oriented organization. The focus of WSLC's training programs, therefore, is to boost the ability of the organization's employees to provide high-quality customer service. In gauging the effects of these efforts, the management team strongly believed that the increased emphasis on training in recent years has improved business results, including the productivity of the organization. WSLC's leadership team also pointed to qualitative measures of the training's impact, including the fact that employees have developed the confidence and understanding they need to take an "invaluable fresh look" at operations and make suggestions for improvement.

Management has adopted a similar view of training at UPMC-Passavant. The theory behind the learning opportunities provided at this organization is simple—employees must have the skills required to provide the highest possible level of care to the patients they treat, and training is an instrument for achieving that goal. Further, in recent years, management at UPMC-Passavant has come to recognize that the quality of the learning opportunities offered at the organization is an important factor in attracting and retaining employees, a view that was confirmed in our interviews with lower-wage workers.

Logistics

No matter how committed an organization's leadership is to the idea of training for all workers, its potential is limited if there is not a similar commitment to adapting that learning to the employees' individual interests, schedules, and needs. Especially for lower-wage workers who have trouble leaving the job site for training, organizations must ensure that employees have ample opportunities and incentives to take advantage of a full menu of training options.

In particular, organizations need to carve out special times for lower-wage workers to engage in training. Seeking to overcome the challenge of serving a staff that works in three shifts running 24 hours a day, the training department at UPMC "markets" itself to all shifts. The training staff goes so far as to conduct surveys to determine what times are most convenient for training sessions, and trainers make a point of being available and offering training during times outside the typical hours of the day shift.

Creating an environment that is flexible enough to promote widespread use of training gets back to the question of leadership. At the manufacturer Lacks Enterprises, we found that some managers were either more willing or more able to arrange work and production schedules so their employees could participate in voluntary on-site training. To the extent that organizational leaders can make this sort of flexibility the norm, they will see higher levels of participation in training and, in turn, better results.

Being flexible is not just a matter of adapting training to employees' schedules. It also requires adapting it to their interests. At many of the organizations we studied, training programs offered voluntary courses in subjects that are keyed as much to employees' personal growth and satisfaction as they are to the specific responsibilities of their jobs. BECU, for example, has adopted the following as the mission of its corporate training department: "Because we believe in the ultimate potential of every employee, we provide opportunities for self-discovery, along with personal and professional growth, that contribute to the overall success of BECU" (BECU 2000). In line with this commitment, BECU offers courses in everything from people skills and stress management to a course entitled "Discover Your Career Path," in addition to the expected courses in job-specific skills.

Similarly, both UPMC-Passavant and MGMC offer a wide variety of courses that are unrelated to any competency requirements. These include courses aimed at providing a better understanding of the health care field, as well as courses in personal development. And, responding to employees' wishes for more help with their computer skills, MGMC's small training staff includes one full-time educator dedicated solely to computer training.

Some degree of financial flexibility also helps organizations to make broad commitments to opportunities for their lower-wage employees. The not-for-profit status of some organizations represents one source of such flexibility. Indeed, this may help to explain the disproportionate representation in the case studies of not-for-profit organizations that are particularly successful in providing lower-wage worker training.[2] While all organizations consider bottom-line financial results to be an important factor, the absence of any need to generate profit still provides more flexibility for not-for-profit organizations, all else being equal. They can more easily, therefore, place a high priority on issues related to employee satisfaction and quality of opportunities.

WHAT ABOUT EMPLOYEE DEMAND?

One general point that emerges from the case studies is that the majority of lower-wage workers wanted workplace training opportunities. Most workers welcomed the opportunities they were provided and expressed a desire for more, often in areas of their personal interest or areas that would enhance their general skills and career prospects. It is important to note, however, that these desires were for employer-provided training occurring primarily during work hours—an absolutely ideal scenario from the perspective of the worker. Even for this category of training, demand was not unanimous. A few workers indicated that they did not see the value of the specific courses that were being offered to them. Others reported that they did not see the value of acquiring additional education. In other words, they saw no possibility that it would result in higher wages or a better job.

Some employees, many of whom were enthusiastic about existing training opportunities, were asked about alternative arrangements to meet their training goals—such as arriving early or staying late to take a course. In general, these employees expressed a relatively low willingness to give up their own time to take advantage of such opportunities. They most often cited duties and obligations outside work, such as family or another job, although inconvenience was also mentioned. To be sure, some employees would have been willing to make sacrifices to receive additional training, but they were the minority among employees with whom this issue was discussed. Notably, having the employees pay for some portion of their training was almost certainly not a realistic possibility.

Overall, therefore, the limited conversations we had with employees regarding the extent of their demand for training opportunities showed us that there was significant, but not universal, demand for the most desirable category of training from the workers' perspective: employer-funded, general skills, typically during the workday. Support diminished when any of those characteristics was missing. Additional research in this area is warranted. Unfortunately, the standard employee interview did not include questions that would have allowed more definitive conclusions on the subject of levels of demand among lower-wage workers for different types of training.

CONCLUSIONS

As our case studies demonstrate, some organizations are indeed making a clear commitment to providing training for lower-wage workers. They may have different motivations and objectives, and their strategies and training programs may vary considerably, but they are investing time and money in finding out what works. And they are learning important lessons that can help other organizations, as well as government agencies and other outside actors, seeking to influence organizational practice in the training field.

Organizational Issues

Among the primary issues that our case studies raise for organizations are leadership commitment and logistics. The organizations that are proving most successful in making training available to lower-wage workers—and seeing clear benefits from that training—are those that have made a top-down (that is, leadership) commitment to organization-wide learning as a cornerstone of their success. As part of that commitment, they recognize the importance of logistics—that is, that their training programs must be administered in such a way that employees are fully able to participate.

Policy-Related Issues

For policymakers and others interested in encouraging more widespread adoption of training for lower-wage workers, the issues are somewhat different. First and foremost, continued work needs to be done in demonstrating learning results—if only to educate more organizations and their employees of the potential payoff that comes with a commitment to training. In addition, our case studies demonstrate that government interventions to promote training for these workers can be effective. Both of the two for-profit firms included in our case-study sample received some form of government assistance for providing or developing training. This suggests that targeted policy interventions at all levels of government can play an important role in encouraging more firms to take action on this issue.

We fully recognize that many, if not all, of the organizations we have studied are "best-case scenarios" in terms of their perspective on training and the benefits of making it available broadly throughout the workforce. We expect that their lessons may provide some other organizations with the motivation to extend training to larger numbers of lower-wage workers.

Note

1. This and other such quotes, both direct and indirect, are taken from our notes made during the various case study interviews.
2. Five of the seven case-study organizations are not-for-profit organizations. For-profit status was not one of the elements on which we screened to determine who would be included in the case studies.

12
Summary and Policy Implications

For a variety of reasons—ranging from the vicissitudes of a tight labor market to a philosophical predisposition—some employers have chosen to make unusual commitments to provide significant education and training opportunities to their lower-wage workforce. Interestingly enough, this commitment rarely manifests itself in a direct focus on lower-wage workers. Instead, we find simply that lower-wage workers in these organizations are not singled out for any unusual treatment. They typically do not receive more or less training than anyone else in the enterprise, but rather are provided with the same access to educational opportunities that is available to all workers throughout the enterprise. This is, in itself, unusual, since most organizations provide disproportionately more training to workers with more education.

Although it is difficult to quantify the benefits of a strategy that provides atypical development opportunities to lower-wage workers, the enterprises that have chosen this path are adamant in their view that it has paid off for them. Most frequently, they point to improvements in employee retention and customer satisfaction as evidence of the payoff to their investments in training for lower-wage employees.

So if there is, in fact, a payoff to this strategy, why don't more firms use it? The employers whom we found pursuing this strategy have discovered that doing so can be good for both their workers and their business. Some employers began this strategy with the intention of doing right by their workers but found that they were also doing well financially as a result. Others pursued it purely from the perspective of the bottom line, but found that the strategy was good for their workers as well. In both cases, these unusual organizations have come to view their lower-wage workers as important assets, worthy of the investment in education and training opportunities. Few employers, however, do choose to make significant investments in their lower-wage workers, perhaps because such a mindset is not commonly found. Lower-wage workers inside our unusual organizations supported this observation when, during interviews, many volunteered that they were treated "like a valuable part of the organization," frequently drawing a contrast with their previous employers. We believe that there are a number of ways in which public policy can help to encourage this perspective, while overcoming additional barriers to training for lower-wage workers.

FINDINGS

Phase 1—Data Analysis

Given the finding that most organizations provide disproportionately less training to lower-wage workers than to other workers, we analyzed the ASTD database in detail to identify what types of organizations are more likely to provide training opportunities to their lower-wage workers. The analysis found that organizations that provide an above-average level of training for such employees are most likely to have between 500 and 2,000 employees. Examined by industry, organizations in health care and those that are family-owned, privately held, or not-for-profit tend to provide more training to lower-wage employees. Somewhat surprisingly, however, the organizations that provided more training to lower-wage workers actually spent less on training per employee and as a percentage of payroll, even though they generally trained a higher percentage of their employees overall. They tended to rely somewhat less on classroom training and to dedicate slightly more resources to new-employee orientation, and they were more likely to use government organizations to deliver training, a point that helped to underscore the results in the third phase of the study.

In terms of learning outcomes, courses whose participants are mostly lower-wage employees were generally evaluated less favorably by their participants immediately following their completion than were other courses. One possible explanation for this finding is that a group of lower-wage workers may consist disproportionately of individuals with a low tolerance for classroom learning (as evidenced by a lower-than-average level of formal education). Interestingly, however, after some time has passed, both participants and their supervisors generally assessed the positive productivity effects of the courses provided to lower-wage workers as having been greater than those of courses provided to higher-wage employees.

Phase 2—Telephone Surveys

The telephone survey component of the analysis showed that there is a wide range of practices and policies with regard to training for lower-wage employees. Some organizations provided the bare minimum of training to their employees; in those, the training required by law was the only training the lower-wage employees ever received. At the other end of the spectrum were organizations (few in number) that have a deeply held belief that training is good. In these organizations, all employees, regardless of their position, received almost the same training, and typically were actively encouraged to seek growth-oriented training opportunities on their own.

The tight labor market at the time of the research definitely affected training practices. Some organizations viewed this market as an opportunity to use training to ensure that their current employees did not leave, while others cut back their training to make sure that production lines did not shut down while employees were away from work to attend training.

Finally, with regard to the technology of training, there is a relatively wide variety of experiences among these organizations in the delivery of training to lower-wage workers. Some reported that electronic learning technologies are a highly effective method for delivering training, while others reported that they have been unsuccessful in using such methods.

Phase 3—Case Studies

The relative dearth of education and training opportunities for lower-wage workers could be the result of limited supply or limited demand. Although there is no precise way, given the available data and research, to determine whether supply or demand is the more constraining factor, the case-study phase of our research did, nonetheless, provide useful insights into this issue.

Although the organizations that were involved in the case-study phase of the work were chosen because of their unusual commitment to training for lower-wage workers, most of them still struggled to find the resources to make training available. We found that, in the area of training for lower-wage workers, commitment meant much more than simply monetary commitment—it also involved actions and culture. Indeed, the primary constraint (at least in this admittedly nonrandom sample of firms) was not budgetary. In other words, the direct cost of training (primarily instructors' salaries) was not the primary resource constraint. The primary constraint was rather the opportunity cost of workers' time. Almost all the case study organizations struggled to find ways to release workers from their jobs so that they could attend classes.

This is a fundamental, and important, conclusion of the study. The type of work that lower-wage workers do—especially in the manufacturing and service sectors—typically requires that they be physically present on a set schedule to accomplish their work. Moreover, that work cannot be deferred to some later time. So when they leave to attend class, the work simply does not get done, and that is costly.

We also encountered evidence that workers' demands for workplace education may in some cases represent a constraining factor. Most workers were enthusiastic about employer-funded training, and expressed a desire for additional opportunities, particularly in areas of interest to them (the most frequently mentioned, computer training, is, of course, a general skill, the primary benefits of which would be expected to accrue over the long term to the employee).

At the same time, however, a smaller number of workers failed to see the value of the courses they were offered or, more generally, the value of additional education. A larger number of employees began to express doubts when presented with scenarios involving greater sacrifice on their parts, even such minimal sacrifice as having voluntary training occur outside of work hours. Still, there were employees who remained positive about such a prospect. In the end, we simply do not have enough information to determine if lower-wage workers' views in this regard differ from higher-wage workers. Research over the past few years (see Chapter 1) has found that, despite the predictions of economic theory, employers typically do finance the costs of general training. Consequently, lower-wage workers' expectations that their employers should bear the (time) costs of training may not be out of line with the norm.

The primary benefit that the case-study organizations attributed to their investments in training for lower-wage workers was an enhanced ability to attract and retain employees, a benefit that was likely related indirectly, if at all, to the content of the training being provided. Although none had quantified the value of this benefit, the organizations were universal in their view that this benefit was significant and substantially exceeded the costs. Most of the case-study organizations also reported that their training investments resulted in improved customer satisfaction or product quality. Again, although none of the organizations had a mechanism for quantifying such a benefit, they were nonetheless certain that the benefit was substantial.

In almost every one of the case-study organizations, it was clear how important it was that the leadership be committed to investing in people, and that its commitment be recognized throughout the organization. It was clear that the commitment needed to be measured not only in dollars, but also in leadership, actions, and culture. As noted earlier, these organizations did not have an investment strategy directed specifically at their lower-wage workers. Rather, they had a strategy for investing in their people, and lower-wage workers received the same level of investment as other workers.

Because most of the case-study organizations were not-for-profit organizations, we conclude that such organizations appear to be able to do a better job of providing learning opportunities to lower-wage workers than do comparable organizations in the for-profit sector. Indeed, both of the for-profit firms among our case-study organizations received substantial grants from state or local government. These grants were clearly important catalysts in the approach to training in these firms.

We reject the conclusion that the absence of unsubsidized for-profit firms among our case-study organizations provides *de facto* evidence that training for lower-wage workers is not—or, perhaps more important, cannot be—profitable. Such a conclusion would logically follow if and only if markets (including the labor market) met all the strict assumptions necessary to generate perfect competition. Since there is ample evidence that markets do not behave according to these textbook-based assumptions, it does not necessarily follow that the lack of training for lower-wage workers in for-profit firms demonstrates that it is not (or cannot be) profitable.

Rather, it is reasonable to conclude that imperfections in the operation of markets constrain employers from making profitable investments in lower-wage workers. The findings from the recent literature on firm-financed general training discussed in Chapter 1, for example, provide *prima facie* evidence of the existence of market imperfections. In this case, the issue then becomes identifying the appropriate role for public policy (see the discussion below).

Finally, the dearth of technology-delivered learning in the case-study organizations was striking. The promise of technology-delivered training—available anytime, anywhere, in any amount, and at low marginal cost—is that it may solve one of the most vexing barriers of expanding education and training opportunities for lower-wage workers: that they must leave their work to attend class. If workers could have access to learning opportunities at will (on lunch breaks, before or after work, or at home), this barrier could become less constraining, at least for those workers interested in pursuing work-related development opportunities during nonwork hours. But while some of the case-study organizations are considering using learning technologies to improve their training, none has yet succeeded in making significant progress in this direction.

IMPLICATIONS FOR EMPLOYERS

Research has shown that firms that make significant investments in education and training enjoy lower employee turnover, higher customer retention, higher rates of innovation, improved financial performance, and higher total stockholder returns (see Bassi, Copeman, and McMurrer 2000). Nonetheless, in the area of workplace education and training there is a wide gulf between the rhetoric—"people are our most important asset"—and the reality. In this domain of human resource management, perhaps more so than elsewhere, many organizations are playing the "new-economy game" by the "old-economy rules." In the new economy, in which human capital is the source of the vast majority of wealth creation, workers are an asset, and education and training is an investment. In the old economy, workers are a cost and so too is their education and training. In the gray area between, workers are proclaimed to be an asset, but education and training continues to be treated as a cost.

The confusion that results from playing the new-economy game by the old-economy rules affects the education and training strategies of most organizations, as well as how those strategies affect workers. The effects are almost certainly the most profound for those workers at the bottom of the pile—those who are the lowest paid and have the least formal education and bargaining power. Even though most employers acknowledge that these workers play an important role in producing satisfied customers and high-quality products, and that they contribute significantly to the bottom line, the evidence clearly indicates that these are the workers who are least likely to be treated as true assets by their employer. Hence, these are the workers in whom employers invest the least. Yet, given the laws of diminishing marginal return, it seems reasonable to expect that effective education and training for lower-wage workers would stand a good chance of generating a positive return on employers' investments, perhaps an even higher return than investments in higher-wage workers.

The fact that employers do not make significant investments in these workers suggests several possibilities: that there are significant barriers to such investments; that there is an information problem in that employers do not know how to invest in lower-wage workers or do not know what the expected returns are; that the potential complexities most uniquely associated with training for lower-wage workers (such as an aversion to classroom training) are sufficiently daunting to discourage it; or that employers' experiences have indicated that such investments are not as cost effective as investments in other categories of workers.

The organizations included in the case-study phase of the research may provide a useful example for other employers considering their training strategy. Generally, as a result of their education and training strategies, the case-study organizations enjoy improved ability to recruit and retain employees and enhanced customer satisfaction. Moreover, they understand that the best strategy for providing education and training to lower-wage workers is to have no special strategy at all. Rather, the best strategy is simply to offer the same learning opportunities to all workers.

IMPLICATIONS FOR EMPLOYEES

The fact that large numbers of working adults are returning to school is testimony to the increasing economic significance of lifelong learning. Many of these adults are pursing this path with the benefit of either tuition reimbursement plans from their employer or direct employer financing of their education. Workplace-based education and training represent an alternative (or complementary) path to school-based adult programs, and in many cases likely represent a more efficient mechanism for adults to participate in lifelong learning and enjoy the economic benefits created. Leading-edge employers are now using such investments in employee education and training to distinguish themselves from other employers, and become "employers of choice."

A great potential benefit of the unfolding of the knowledge era is that lifelong learning is one of those rare areas in which the interests of employers and employees can nearly entirely coincide, resulting in increased productivity for employers and increased earnings capacity for employees. This suggests that employers' fledgling efforts to compete for employees on the "fringe benefit" aspects of workplace education and training are likely to increase in the years to come, and spread to broader categories of workers. We would expect that employees from an increasingly broad spectrum of the skill and wage distribution (that is, not just those at the top) will come to demand such benefits from employers.

IMPLICATIONS FOR PUBLIC POLICY

Economic theory predicts that firms will typically not invest in workers' "general skills"—those that are highly portable and of value to a wide variety of employers. And although this prediction relies on strong assumptions (which are almost certainly unrealistic), there is insight in it nonetheless. The skills that have the broadest applicability and are, therefore, arguably of greatest value—to both workers and employers—are paradoxically the skills in which employers will be least likely to invest. Moreover, the workers that would stand to benefit the most from these skills—those with the least formal education and skills—are precisely the workers in whom employers are the least likely to invest.

In a textbook model of the world, none of this would be problematic. Workers would simply invest in themselves—either directly or indirectly—by accepting lower wages in exchange for "employer-provided" education (which, according to the theory, would be "financed" through wage reductions). The world does not, however, operate according to this textbook model.[1] And because of that, there is a role for public policy to play in promoting workplace education and training, particularly for the most economically disadvantaged members of the workforce—those who have the fewest resources available to invest in their own education and training.

At the most fundamental level, there are only two categories of policies that the government can pursue to create incentives for employers to provide more education and training to lower-wage workers. The first category of policies helps reduce employers' costs, and the second helps identify and improve the benefits that result from investments in education and training.

Reducing Costs

With regard to costs, there are three strategies that public policy can and should use:

1) Public policy should help *reduce the fixed (start-up) costs* associated with providing education and training for lower-wage workers. Various means might include facilitating the creation of consortia of employers to work together to develop an educational content or curriculum that is broadly applicable and can be shared. Some of this curriculum would be industry specific, in which case working in collaboration with industry associations might be a promising approach.

2) It should *subsidize the marginal costs* of delivering highly portable skills to lower-wage workers. Since employers will most likely fail to provide optimal levels of highly portable, basic skills to lower-wage workers, this is the area in which public policy should focus most intensely on reducing employers' costs. (Spill-

over effects that create positive externalities argue for intervention with regard to basic skills for adults.) Such subsidies could take the form of underwriting "employer-provided" courses in general educational development (GED) preparation, English as a second language, and other basic skills development initiatives.

3) And it should help *make workplace education more accessible* (from the perspectives of both employers and lower-wage employees) by subsidizing the creation of a relevant curriculum that can be more easily built into work or made more convenient for employees. This includes, but is not limited to, learning that is delivered electronically. A strategy focused on electronic delivery holds the promise for dramatically reducing the direct costs (both fixed and marginal) associated with workplace education and training, as well as the opportunity costs (the value of lost productivity). Reducing the opportunity costs, in turn, could help solve one of the most fundamental barriers that employers face in providing education for lower-wage workers—finding ways to release them from work to attend class. Asynchronous learning, which workers can take at their convenience (as opposed to when the class is being held), holds the promise of ameliorating the requirement that workers be released from work to attend class.

Identifying Benefits

Public policy also needs to be involved in measuring and determining the benefits of various forms of training. A primary obstacle that proponents of workplace education for lower-wage workers often face is demonstrating the economic value—the benefit—that is produced by firms' investments. The absence of agreed-upon methods for measuring and valuing firms' investments in education and training is a central part of this problem.

A second, and closely related, obstacle results from the fact that training is currently accounted for as a cost, and there are no public reporting requirements associated with it. Consequently, publicly traded firms are penalized by financial markets (at least in the short run) when they spend money on training, since doing so increases the apparent operating costs without any future benefit that is discernable to investors (see Bassi et al. 2000; Bassi et al. 2001).

We strongly believe that this is one of the reasons why not-for-profit and family owned organizations provide more training to lower-wage workers than do for-profit firms. Because these organizations need not publicly submit their costs (which include the hidden, unmeasured investment that training represents) on a quarterly basis for the scrutiny of Wall Street, they are immune from the perverse investment disincentives that such scrutiny creates.

There are two relatively low-cost public policy vehicles that government should use to help solve these problems:

1) Government should facilitate the creation of standardized systems for measuring the economic impact of employers' investments in education and training. ASTD's Benchmarking Service (which includes standardized measures of benefits and has already been partly subsidized by the U.S. Department of Labor) is an example of the type of assistance that could help in this regard.

2) From an accounting and reporting perspective, firms' investments in education and training need to be put on an equal footing with other strategic investments (such as capital spending and research and development). Government should be actively exploring the changes that are necessary in how firms are required to account for and report on their investments in people so that financial markets stop penalizing and begin encouraging such investments.[2]

THE NEED FOR ADDITIONAL RESEARCH

Finally, government has a role to play in financing the research necessary to provide additional policy guidance.

A guiding principle for research on workplace training, and most particularly how it relates to lower-wage workers, should be to identify and quantify market imperfections that prevent otherwise profitable investments from being made. It would be particularly instructive if future research were to focus on identifying the following:

- What barriers are particularly relevant in constraining the amount of employer-provided training that is made available to lower-wage workers?

- What financial benefits (if any) accrue to those employers that learn to overcome those barriers?

- And what are the most cost-effective methods available to enhance the quantity and quality of education and training available to the least advantaged members of the workforce?

Notes

1. If the world did operate according to the theory, then investments in workplace education would simply generate an "average" market return. These investments, however, appear to generate above-average returns. (For evidence on this, see, for example, Frazis and Loewenstein 1999.) This suggests that, left to its own means, the market would invest too little in workplace education and training, or that there are other nonfinancial costs that need to be taken into consideration.

2. A report recently released by the Brookings Institution (Blair and Wallman 2001) provides specific guidance on this issue.

Appendix A

INTRODUCTORY COMMENTS

As part of a grant from the Ford Foundation and Upjohn Institute for Employment Research, the American Society for Training and Development (ASTD) is gathering information on employer-provided training for lower-wage employees. We greatly appreciate your agreeing to participate in this project.

Any information that you give us will be kept anonymous and will not be attributed to you or your organization without your permission. If you don't have any objections, I will be recording our conversation to help me write up my notes after this interview. Thanks.

For all of the questions that follow, we're primarily interested in the experience of your organization over the last few years, from 1997 to the present.

If, as we go through the questions, there are any for which you think it would be useful for us to talk to someone else in your organization, please feel free to let me know.

We're trying to understand training for people without basic workplace skills and/or people earning lower wages. There's really no precise definition for this group, so for the purposes of this survey we'll define the group that we're interested in as the following: It contains those employees who are 1) paid on an hourly basis and 2) earn less than $10 per hour. I'll use the term "lower-wage employees" throughout the questions to refer to anyone in this general category.

Before we start, what part of your organization do you feel qualified to discuss: your entire company, this location, several locations, a business unit, a division, or something else? This will be referred to as "your organization" for the remainder of the survey.

SURVEY QUESTIONS

A. Lower-Wage Employees in the Organization

1) What percentage of your organization would you say is currently made up of lower-wage employees?

2) Are your lower-wage employees concentrated in certain parts or areas of your organization? (Certain jobs, regions, business units, overseas, etc.)

3) Has your organization seen any change in the proportion of lower-wage employees in your organization (relative to other employees)?

> *If yes:* About what percentage of your workforce in 1997 fell into this category?
>
> What is the main reason for the change from 1997?

B. Content of Training Provided

1) On what topics do most lower-wage employees in your organization receive training? (*Prompt to make sure respondent lists all areas that are typically provided to lower-wage employees.*)

> *If confusion about content types, provide the ASTD categories:* Basic skills; occupational safety/compliance; customer relations; information technology skills; technical processes; sales/dealer; product knowledge; business practices; interpersonal communication; employee orientation; professional skills; managerial; executive development.

2) Overall, approximately what percentage of the training time of lower-wage employees would you say falls into each of three broad categories that I'm going to list? 1) *work-related* skills development, 2) *personal* skills development, or 3) other training generally required for most or all of your organization? (*Should add to 100%—if less, ask if there's some portion of the training that doesn't fall into any of these categories.*)

C. Amount of Training Provided

1) Have you in any way tracked the amount of training your organization is providing to lower-wage employees?

> *If yes:* What do you keep track of? (Expenditures, time, etc.)
>
> Has it increased or decreased since 1997? (Details.)
>
> *If respondent was Measurement Kit participant.*
>
> In your response to the [1999/1998] ASTD *Measurement Kit*, you were asked about the percentage of your total training expenditures that goes to training for employees who have less than 12 years of education. For the 1998 fiscal year, you responded ____% (fill in for each organization). Is this number accurate?

D. How Is Training Delivered?

1) Where do lower-wage employees generally receive their training? (Prompt if necessary: on-site, off-site, etc.)

2) When do lower-wage employees generally receive their training? (Prompt if necessary: during work hours, after work, during lunch, etc.)

3) Have you used any types of technology to deliver training to your lower-wage employees?

> *If yes*:   What types of technology?
> For what types of training do you use this technology?

E. Incentives for Training

1) What types of your training for lower-wage employees are typically mandatory?

2) Are there any specific incentives for lower-wage employees to participate in voluntary training? (Prompt if necessary: required for promotion, required for pay increase, some form of certification, etc.)

3) What is the participation rate in voluntary training initiatives for lower-wage employees? (Can be different for different content categories.)

4) Have you received any feedback on the reasons that lower-wage employees participate in training? What do they say is the primary benefit of the training?

5) What is the primary way your organization benefits from training lower-wage employees?

F. Responsibilities for Training

1) Who is responsible for ensuring that training is provided to lower-wage employees? What part of the organization? Is this the same area responsible for training for other employees?

2) What part of your organization sets or holds the budget for this training?

G. Differences with Other Training

1) Is the training offered to lower-wage employees different in any way from the training offered to other employees in your organization? (For example, you might use particular course delivery techniques, limit training to certain categories, not provide training at all, etc.)

> *If yes*:   Is there a specific group of lower-wage employees for which it is different?
> How is this group defined?
> What is the main difference? (Ineligible, specialized training, more/less training than average, only certain types of training—which—etc.)
> What is the primary reason for training for this difference?

H. Enablers/Barriers

1) Can you name one or two specific factors that make it difficult to provide training for lower-wage employees?

If yes: What are they?
How have you attempted to overcome these difficulties? Have you been successful?

If no: Many organizations report difficulties in providing training for lower-wage employees. Why do you think you have been able to avoid most of those difficulties?

2) Would you like to be able to provide more training to your lower-wage employees?

If yes: What types of training?

I. Effects of Tight Labor Market and Other Factors

1) Has your training for lower-wage employees changed as a result of the increasingly tight labor market?

If yes: What is the primary way your training has changed? (Prompt if necessary: more training for lower-wage employees, different types of training offered, etc.)
Would you expect that these changes would remain in place if the labor market were to loosen in the future? Why? (Details.)

2) Can you think of any other factor or factors that have caused your training for lower-wage employees to change over time? (Prompt if necessary: increased use of technology, globalization, employee turnover, etc.)

If yes: What factor or factors?
What was its biggest impact on your training?

J. Training Evaluation

1) Have you in any way assessed the impact of training for lower-wage employees or related job categories?

If yes: How? (Formal evaluation, other.)
What types of training seem to yield particularly good results?
What types seem to yield particularly poor results?

K. Other Comments

1) That covers all the questions about lower-wage worker training that I wanted to ask you. Do you have any other comments on the issue of training for lower-wage employees?

2) Is there anything else you would like to add before we finish?

L. Other Organizations

1) Before we end, are you aware of any other organizations that you think we should contact because they have been particularly active in training lower-wage employees?

If yes: What is the name of the organization?
Where are they located?
Is there any particular contact person you know whom we should talk to?
May we say that you referred us to them?

CONCLUDING QUESTIONS

1) If we should decide to use some excerpts from this interview in our final report, may we come back to you for your permission?

2) Would you be willing to have the name of your organization listed as one of the participants in this research in our final report?

3) Thank you for your help. We'll send a copy of the final report to you when it is finished. (Confirm address.)

Appendix B

Case Studies—General Framework for On-Site Interviews

BACKGROUND

The case studies included two different sets of on-site interviews: 1) those with representatives of the organization's management, and 2) those with its lower-wage workers. Each case study lasted one day, divided relatively evenly between the two sets.

Management

The management interviews were designed to include at least two different people or groups of people (others were also included at some organizations):

1) The chief executive officer or the vice president of human resources—the person who likely made more general budget decisions than those for just the training budget, and who had a viewpoint of the organization as a whole, rather than just of the training department; and

2) The original contact person (typically a training manager)—the person who was most directly involved with the planning and communicating of the training opportunities provided to lower-wage employees.

Lower-Wage Workers

We requested that the employee interviews take place in a series of 8 to 12 individual conversations with lower-wage workers (or, in one case, with a focus group of such individuals). We requested that the organizations select individuals with a variety of characteristics on the following variables:

1) Occupation—if there was more than one category with a large concentration of lower-wage employees, at least two from each category to be included in the interviews

2) Relatively new hires instead of more tenured employees

3) If there were voluntary training opportunities, people who took advantage of these opportunities rather than those who did not

4) If there was a unionized workforce, both union and nonunion employees

QUESTION FRAMEWORK: MANAGEMENT

Questions for CEO or Vice President

1) What is your organizational mission? Has it changed in the past few years?

   If yes: What was your previous mission and why did you change it?

2) Where does the Education and Training function fit into your organization? How is the training and education department funded? (Attempt to gauge interest in or prioritization of the training function within the organization. Also seek historical perspective.)

> Has there been a recent "push" to expand, initiate, or improve training programs across some or all levels of the organization?
> Has the training budget changed significantly over the past few years?

3) *If training is available for all employees*: What made you decide to offer broad-based training across your workforce when so many other organizations do not? And what factors made this succeed here that may not exist everywhere?

4) What benefits does your organization receive for providing training to lower-wage employees? Are these the benefits you expected to receive from the training? How do you know (measure) what the benefits are? What are they worth?

> *If benefits haven't been realized*: Why not? Do you expect them to be realized in the future?

5) Do you link training to its business outcomes? If so, is doing so necessary to maintain buy-in into training? Do you stop providing training when no link to business outcomes is found?

6) With regard to the training your organization provides to lower-wage workers, what positive and negative effects have you seen from this training in terms of culture, skills, productivity, worker retention, satisfaction, etc.? (*Seek concrete examples.*)

7) How do you get the whole organization to recognize the importance of training your entire staff? Have you needed to use any tactics to "sell" the necessity of providing training to lower-wage employees to managers or supervisors?

> What tactics have you used?
> Are there different techniques to achieve managerial buy-in into training that is mandatory/regulated, organization-specific, or voluntary?

8) How does the organization encourage lower-wage employees to participate in training?

9) How has today's labor market affected the training you provide to lower-wage employees?

10) Have you seen any changes in your entry-level workforce (level of education, salary expectation, quality of work)?

> *If yes*: How have these changes affected your training?

11) Has it been more difficult to retain employees in the past few years?

If yes: Do you plan on using your training program to address that issue?

Questions for Director of Training

1) *Discussion of nature of training*: Much of this information was already collected in the telephone survey. Follow-up based on previous responses, with focus on some of the more interesting or notable forms or methods of training at this organization.

2) Is training available for all lower-wage workers, or only certain groups?

If only certain groups: How are they selected?

3) What types of training do you provide to your lower-wage employees? (*Consult telephone survey results.*) Do you have a tuition reimbursement program?

4) What is the relative breakdown of voluntary versus mandatory training? What are the different objectives of these types of training? What is the take-up rate of voluntary training? What incentives do you have in place to encourage employees to take advantage of voluntary training?

5) What kinds of on-the-job (OJT) training programs have been implemented? (*Seek information on degree of formalization. Seek more complete explanations of any OJT that we might witness while on site.*)

6) Are there any programs that provide transferable or cross-occupational skills? How did such programs come into being?

7) How is training delivered? How frequently? When? Where?

8) If you were redesigning your training programs for lower-wage workers, what might you do differently? What advice can you give to other organizations from your experiences?

9) What kinds of technology are used to provide training?

10) When were these technologies acquired? Was it difficult to convince the necessary people that the investments in these technologies were worthwhile?

11) Have they been successful additions to the training of lower-wage employees? Are there any challenges in providing training through technology that are specific to this group of employees? What do you think are the employees' perceptions of the use of this technology?

12) In what technology would you like to invest more in the future?

13) Do you outsource training for lower-wage employees? Why or why not?

    If no: Would you outsource if you found a company that had the adequate technical expertise for your training requirements?

14) Do you collaborate with other institutions to provide this training? If so, how did this collaboration come about?

15) What benefits does your organization receive for providing training to lower-wage employees? Are these the benefits you expected to receive from the training?

    How do you know (measure) what the benefits are? What are they worth? If benefits haven't been realized, why not? Do you expect them to be realized in the future?

16) Do you feel that your organization's culture and leadership support behavior that is enthusiastic toward the training of lower-wage employees?

17) What problems have been encountered with lower-wage worker training in particular? How were these problems resolved, or are there still problems?

    Have you needed to use any tactics to "sell" the necessity of providing training to lower-wage employees to managers or supervisors? Or have you needed to spend considerable effort in getting employees to buy into training?

    If yes: What tactics have you used?

            Are there different techniques to achieve buy-in into training that is mandatory or regulated, organization-specific, or voluntary?

18) Do you link training to business outcomes?

    If yes: Is doing so necessary to maintain buy-in into training?

19) What do you perceive to be the motivation level of employees participating in training?

20) How do you think your employees feel about the managerial backing behind their training?

21) Can you comment on the extent to which the organization's training of lower-wage employees is seen as good public relations?

22) Are there differences in the training provided to lower-wage employees and training opportunities given to other employees? If so, how do you think lower-wage employees perceive these differences?

23) What positive and negative effects have you seen from these training opportunities in terms of culture, skills, productivity, worker retention, satisfac-

tion, etc.? (*Concrete examples.*) Within this wage group in particular, has your organization faced employee retention difficulties?

24) What lessons could others learn from your experiences with training this group of employees?

QUESTION FRAMEWORK: LOWER-WAGE WORKERS

1) How long have you been working at Company X? Do you anticipate a long future with Company X?

2) What positions have you held?

If more than one: Was the decision to change positions initiated by you or by the organization?

3) Can you describe the typical career path or length of stay of people in your position?

4) What types of training have you received in order to perform your current job? (New hire orientation, technical skills, basic skills, OJT.) Have you progressed through a series of courses, or have various courses qualified you to do different jobs?

5) Do you feel you have access to the training that is necessary for you to complete your job? If access is an issue, how could the situation be improved?

6) Is access distributed evenly among employees? Who has access?

7) Have you witnessed changes in the way training is delivered in the organization?

8) How much of your training has been OJT training?

9) Are you provided with opportunities to receive education that is not specifically applicable to your job? (For example, does your organization have a tuition reimbursement policy?) How do you learn about these opportunities? Do you take part in them?

If yes: What kinds of opportunities are offered?
Do these opportunities fit into your schedule? Are they during work hours? If so, do you get paid time to take these opportunities? What goes into your decision as to whether or not to take advantage of these opportunities?
Do you feel that these opportunities exist elsewhere, but just not within Company X?

If the worker hasn't taken advantage of voluntary opportunities:
Did you know about _____ opportunity? (*Specify.*)

What did you think about this option?
Was it a good idea? Why didn't you participate?
Was it a waste of time? Why?

10) How would you characterize the culture of this organization? Are your managers supportive of the training you take part in? What types of incentives do you have for participating in training? Can you talk to me a little bit about the turnover/retention of your coworkers?

References

American Society for Training and Development (ASTD). 1997. *Measurement Kit: Parts I and II*. Alexandria, VA: ASTD.

———. 1998. *Measurement Kit: Parts I and II*. Alexandria, VA: ASTD.

Barron, John M., Mark C. Berger, and Dan A. Black. 1997. "How Well Do We Measure Training?" *Journal of Human Resources* 15(3): 507–528.

———. 1999. "Do Workers Pay for On-the-Job Training?" *Journal of Human Resources* 34(2): 235–252.

Bartel, Ann P. 1995. "Training, Wage Growth, and Job Performance: Evidence from a Company Database." *Journal of Labor Economics* 13(3): 401–425.

Bassi, Laurie J. 2000. "Workers at Risk" Working paper, Russell Sage Foundation, New York.

Bassi, Laurie J., Don Copeman, and Daniel P. McMurrer. 2000. "The Business of Learning." White paper. Redwood Shores, CA: Saba Software.

Bassi, Laurie J., Paul Harrison, Jens Ludwig, and Daniel P. McMurrer. 2001. "Human Capital Investments and Firm Performance." White paper. Washington, DC: Georgetown University.

Bassi, Laurie J., Jens Ludwig, Daniel McMurrer, and Mark Van Buren. 2000. "Profiting from Learning." White paper. Redwood Shores, CA: Saba Software.

Bassi, Laurie J., and Mark Van Buren. 1999. "The 1999 ASTD State of the Industry Report." ASTD, Alexandria, VA.

Becker, Gary S. 1962. "Investment in Human Capital: A Theoretical Analysis." *Journal of Political Economy* 70(5): 9–49.

Blair, Margaret, and Steven Wallman. 2001. *Unseen Wealth*. Washington, DC: Brookings Institution.

Boeing Employees' Credit Union (BECU). 2000. "Corporate Training Department: Mission Statement." Unpublished, provided to authors July 2000.

Central Florida Regional Transportation Authority (LYNX). 2000. "Mission Statement." Unpublished, provided to authors July 2000.

Frazis, Harley, Maury Gittleman, Michael Horrigan, and Mary Joyce. 1998. "Results from the 1995 Survey of Employer-Provided Training." *Monthly Labor Review* 121(6): 3–13.

Frazis, Harley, and Mark A. Loewenstein. 1999. *Reexamining the Returns to Training: Functional Form, Magnitude, and Interpretation*. Working paper no. 325, Bureau of Labor Statistics, Washington, DC.

Kirkpatrick, Donald. 1998. *Evaluating Training Programs: The Four Levels.* San Francisco: Berrett-Koehler.

Loewenstein, Mark A., and James R. Spletzer. 1998. "Dividing the Costs and Returns to General Training." *Journal of Labor Economics* 16(1): 142–171.

———. 1999. "General and Specific Training: Evidence and Implications." *Journal of Human Resources* 34(4): 710–733.

Mincer, Jacob. 1989. "Human Capital and the Labor Market: A Review of Current Research." *Educational Researcher* 18(4): 27–34.

Wyoming Student Loan Corporation (WSLC). 2000. "Mission Statement." Unpublished, provided to authors July 2000.

The Authors

Amanda L. Ahlstrand is a management analyst in the Performance and Results Office in the U.S. Department of Labor's Employment and Training Administration (ETA). Prior to joining this office, she worked as a senior public policy research analyst at DTI Associates, where she worked in the General Services Division, providing technical assistance to training and other workforce-related programs. At ETA, DTI, and while working as an analyst at the U.S. General Accounting Office, she has focused on analyzing the performance measures required under Title I of the *Workforce Investment Act of 1998* (Public Law 105-220). She previously held a research associate position at the American Society for Training and Development (ASTD), where she conducted research for this book and helped manage ASTD's Benchmarking Service database. She holds a B.A. from the University of Notre Dame and an M.P.P. from Georgetown University.

Laurie J. Bassi is a labor economist whose career has spanned the academic, not-for-profit, government, and private sectors. She is chief executive officer of Human Capital Capability, Inc., a research-based consulting firm, and the chair of Knowledge Asset Management, Inc., a firm that pursues a strategy of investing in companies that themselves invest significantly in their human capital. Recently, she served as the director of research at Saba Software and the vice president for research at ASTD. She has been a tenured professor of economics and public policy at Georgetown University and has served as the executive director of the Advisory Council on Unemployment Compensation at the U.S. Department of Labor. Her publications and research interests include issues associated with job training for welfare workers, school-to-work programs, the effectiveness of both public and private sector training initiatives, child support, and unemployment compensation. She holds a Ph.D. from Princeton University.

Daniel P. McMurrer is chief research officer at Knowledge Asset Management, Inc., and vice president for research at Human Capital Capability, Inc. Previously, he was a research manager at Saba Software and at ASTD, where his research focused on measuring workplace investments in education and training, and analyzing their effects on financial performance. He also worked at the Urban Institute, where his book, *Getting Ahead: Economic and Social Mobility in America* (co-authored with Isabel Sawhill), was published in 1998. He holds a B.A. from Princeton University and an M.P.P. from Georgetown University.

Index

The italic letters *n* and *t* following a page number indicate that the subject information of the heading is within a note or table, respectively, on that page.

Lemforder Corporation, 18*n*3
Lessons learned from case studies, phase
    3 of current research, 8, 121–133
    barriers to training low-wage
        workers, 125–128, 138
    outstanding issues, 132–133
    reasons to train low-wage workers,
        121–125, 131
    strategies to overcome those training
        barriers, 128–130, 141, 144
    See also under Case studies on
        workplace training, current
        research findings
Logistics to overcome training barriers,
    129–130, 132
Long Beach Transit (firm), 18*n*3
Lower-wage Training Intensive (LWTI)
    firms
    benefits to, from training workers,
        44–45, 138–139
    characteristics of, 21, 22*t*, 49
    course work and (*see main headings,*
        Course evaluations; Courses
        offered)
    current research and, 13, 14, 20–25,
        29*n*3
    instructional methods used by, 23,
        23*t*, 24*t*, 25, 43–44, 46–47, 70,
        87, 100 (*see also* On-the-job
        training (OJT))
    measures of, 22–24*tt*, 139
    workforce size in, 15*t*, 22*t*, 33*t*, 136
    See also Case studies on workplace
        training, current research;
        Workers, low-wage
Lubbock, Texas, 18*n*3
Lucent Technologies/Cirent
    Semiconductor, 18*n*3
LWTI. *See* Lower-wage Training
    Intensive (LWTI) firms
LYNX—The Central Florida Regional
    Transportation Authority, 85–91
    challenges faced, 85, 89

current research at Orlando site, 15*t*,
    18*n*3
education and training initiatives of,
    87–88
employee perspectives, 89–90
lessons learned, 90–91, 123, 126
management perspectives, 89
workforce at, 86–87

Management, 24*t*, 70, 72
    approval by, for employees'
        development plans, 39, 59, 82
    buy-in to training themes, 33–34,
        34*t*, 35*t*, 42, 46, 84
    evaluation of post-training workers
        by, 26, 27*t*, 28, 44, 60
    leadership practiced by, 95–96, 103,
        115, 122, 132
    reluctance to provide human capital
        investment, 126–127, 138
    role in on-site interviews, 16–17,
        153–157
    work-related skill training popular
        with, 60, 82–83
Manufacturing sector
    characteristics of, 32, 33*t*, 38, 42
    competition in, 78, 127
    current research participants in, 15*t*,
        18*n*3, 77–84
    training in, 22*t*, 35*t*, 46, 138
Market-driven businesses, 40
    employers' perspective on training
        in, 33, 35–37*t*, 45, 47
    high turnover and Vista in, 69, 72
    management buy-in for training in,
        34, 35*t*, 46
    training content for different groups
        of workers, 41–43
    training motivation in, 31–32, 33*t*,
        41, 44
Marketing, course offering, 113, 114
Mary Greeley Medical Center (MGMC),
    93–108
    challenges faced by, 93–96

About the Institute

The W.E. Upjohn Institute for Employment Research is a nonprofit research organization devoted to finding and promoting solutions to employment-related problems at the national, state, and local levels. It is an activity of the W.E. Upjohn Unemployment Trustee Corporation, which was established in 1932 to administer a fund set aside by the late Dr. W.E. Upjohn, founder of The Upjohn Company, to seek ways to counteract the loss of employment income during economic downturns.

The Institute is funded largely by income from the W.E. Upjohn Unemployment Trust, supplemented by outside grants, contracts, and sales of publications. Activities of the Institute comprise the following elements: 1) a research program conducted by a resident staff of professional social scientists; 2) a competitive grant program, which expands and complements the internal research program by providing financial support to researchers outside the Institute; 3) a publications program, which provides the major vehicle for disseminating the research of staff and grantees, as well as other selected works in the field; and 4) an Employment Management Services division, which manages most of the publicly funded employment and training programs in the local area.

The broad objectives of the Institute's research, grant, and publication programs are to 1) promote scholarship and experimentation on issues of public and private employment and unemployment policy, and 2) make knowledge and scholarship relevant and useful to policymakers in their pursuit of solutions to employment and unemployment problems.

Current areas of concentration for these programs include causes, consequences, and measures to alleviate unemployment; social insurance and income maintenance programs; compensation; workforce quality; work arrangements; family labor issues; labor-management relations; and regional economic development and local labor markets.